SPARTANAT
RED BOOK

3

SPARTANAT

www.spartanat.com

ISBN: 978-3-903526-12-9

COMBAT EXPERIENCE

MILITARY LESSONS FROM THE WAR IN UKRAINE

CHRISTIAN VÄTH

CONTENTS

STRATEGIC FACTORS

TACTICAL FACTORS

"As long as I'm healthy, I'll keep fighting. I can carry an assault rifle or a machine gun. I spent four months last winter actively engaged in combat using a PKM machine-gun. What else is a man supposed to do? He defends his country. As simple as that."

"Grandpa", 71 years old, mortar squad leader of a volunteer militia in March 2023

FOREWORD

Whether in ancient times or today, there are factors that have always influenced the course of war in very similar ways. This included the will to fight and the willingness to kill—or be killed. Neither can be purchased, and both are difficult to grasp. A country can invest a large part of its economic output in armaments and still be defeated if its people are not prepared to fight. But where does this will come from? Military science has been trying to answer this question for centuries—and yet they have only succeeded in retrospect and in individual cases. What is certain is that armed conflict within one's own species is part of human nature—regardless of whether or not one likes it.

At all levels, individuals utilize psychology in war. People can declare any facet of life as a reason for war. It is also certain that demonizing and dehumanizing the enemy increases people's willingness to kill. Another constant is the disillusionment with the harsh and ugly reality of the craft of war, which always sets in when the not uncommon initial euphoria evaporates. In the end, there is always sadness for losses and regret for missed opportunities, but sometimes also triumph.

Finally, there is also no question of how much war can focus the creativity of individuals and groups. Individuals and groups have developed or adapted countless technological achievements for combat use. However, there is always the ultimate risk because the final outcome is unforeseeable, and all too often, the unthinkable can happen. It's like B.H. Liddell-Hart, one of the most brilliant theorists on the phenomenon of war, once stated: "War is like a boxing match against an unknown person in complete darkness."

Since the victor always sees 'success', judging who is truly ready for war, when, and in what context becomes difficult. Wars are determined by so many factors that although they may be similar, they are never the same. What works in Ukraine today may be a mistake somewhere else tomorrow. It is crucial not to measure your readiness for war by your ability to fight the last war, but the next one. To date, this method still has a considerable margin of error. The Ukrainian people have passed the first part of this stress test in a way that few would have thought possible. The author's prediction at the start of the war also (fortunately) did not come true. The defense against Russian aggression in the first year of the war is a remarkable military achievement, but blatant mistakes also made it possible on the part of the enemy. Perhaps the most important lesson for European societies is the complete surprise of a foreseeable escalation. There is currently a shift in thinking towards greater defense readiness in many nations.

Since February 2022, commentators of all stripes have been inundating the public with verbose assessments of the military capabilities of the two warring parties in Eastern Europe. Everyone's been discussing how to wage war lately. What was previously only observed in football is now also a reality in combat: so-called experts suddenly appear everywhere. Fortunately, among these countless voices there are now more and more real experts, such as Colonel Markus Reisner.

The author has made it his mission to provide the layperson with the basic knowledge and the expert with useful discussion topics. Writing about an ongoing conflict is risky, because no one knows how or when the war will end. Knowing full well that only well-founded assumptions can be made, especially due to the lack of reliable information, one or two statements in this work will certainly be refuted or need to be updated in the coming years. Above all, the interested readers have in their hands a snapshot that should encourage them to take a more balanced view of the mechanics and realities of war than is given in many media outlets.

The work does not claim to be complete and is written with humility for the people who are fighting this war and cannot currently afford the luxury of writing. War is scary, cruel, dirty, ugly, exhausting—and yet sometimes also right. Since today, thanks to deep fakes and omnipresent propaganda, you can almost never be sure whether you are seeing what is true or being plated; it is even more important to remember one thing: evil exists in all of us. To consciously decide against it and stand up for freedom is a sign of strength and will.

So, despite the severity of the topic, I hope the reader finds the read profitable and that we can all be spared another global conflagration.

The war in Ukraine—here a soldier in the destroyed city of Mariupol—took Europe by surprise. It presented the pacifist continent with an image of full-scale war that many had believed would never happen again on European soil.

THE MORNING-AFTER BLUES

AN ASSESSMENT OF THE SITUATION BY MARKUS REISNER

How the war in Ukraine will continue in 2024 depends primarily on the support of the "West", primarily the USA and the EU, for Ukraine. Perhaps it would be better–although not entirely geographically correct–to speak of the "global north", since in addition to China, many states in the "global south" tend to support the Russian position here.

Russia is entering 2024 with a very high level of self-confidence and hopes to achieve further decisive– especially military–successes in the next few months. Russia is increasingly convinced that it can compete with the "global north" in terms of staying power. The year 2024 is an important election year, and not just in the USA. In this context, Russia expects these elections will strengthen forces that are opposed to further support for Ukraine. Therefore, they believe they have just to hold out until the predicted election outcome. Putin sees himself on the winning road, which makes negotiations unnecessary at this point. It's just a matter of following this path to the end, despite all the losses. Putin also looks forward to his own election in 2024 with confidence. The general

Russian population appears to be actively embracing the official narrative of the Ukraine War being "The Great Patriotic War 2.0".

The year 2024 will therefore be the culmination point in the Ukraine war, i.e. the support measures taken or not taken in the next few months will decide whether Ukraine and thus also the "global north" win or lose against Russia. Apart from the upcoming presidential election with an uncertain outcome, the USA is also becoming more distracted by other conflicts and challenges. The maritime alliance in the Red Sea to protect one of the world's most important trade routes, military and financial support from Israel, increasing attacks on US bases in Iraq and Syria, the Taiwan problem and the question of border policy with Mexico are all pushing for solutions . In addition, the majority of US citizens still seem to have little interest in foreign policy issues.

This means that the Europeans are called upon to take on a larger and, above all, more pioneering role in the Ukrainian war. However, there is no evidence of an implementation of the much-quoted "turning point," to use this term that was coined with enthusiasm in Germany. If you want to prevent Russia from gaining the momentum in 2024, i.e. not only keeping the occupied Ukrainian territories, but even expanding its conquests that violate international law, then action must be taken quickly and decisively. If this does not happen, there is a risk of a "frozen" situation analogous to the Korean War, including an "Iron Curtain 2.0" or, in the event of further significant losses of territory, even a massive defeat for Ukraine.

RUSSIA'S WAR IN UKRAINE
from February 24, 2022 until summer 2024

BELARUS

POLAND

KYIV

U K R A

MOLDOVA

ROMANIA

Ukraine

Recaptured Ukrainian territory

Ukrainian territories occupied by Russia

The front line on an animated map:
https://tinyurl.com/ywae3av5

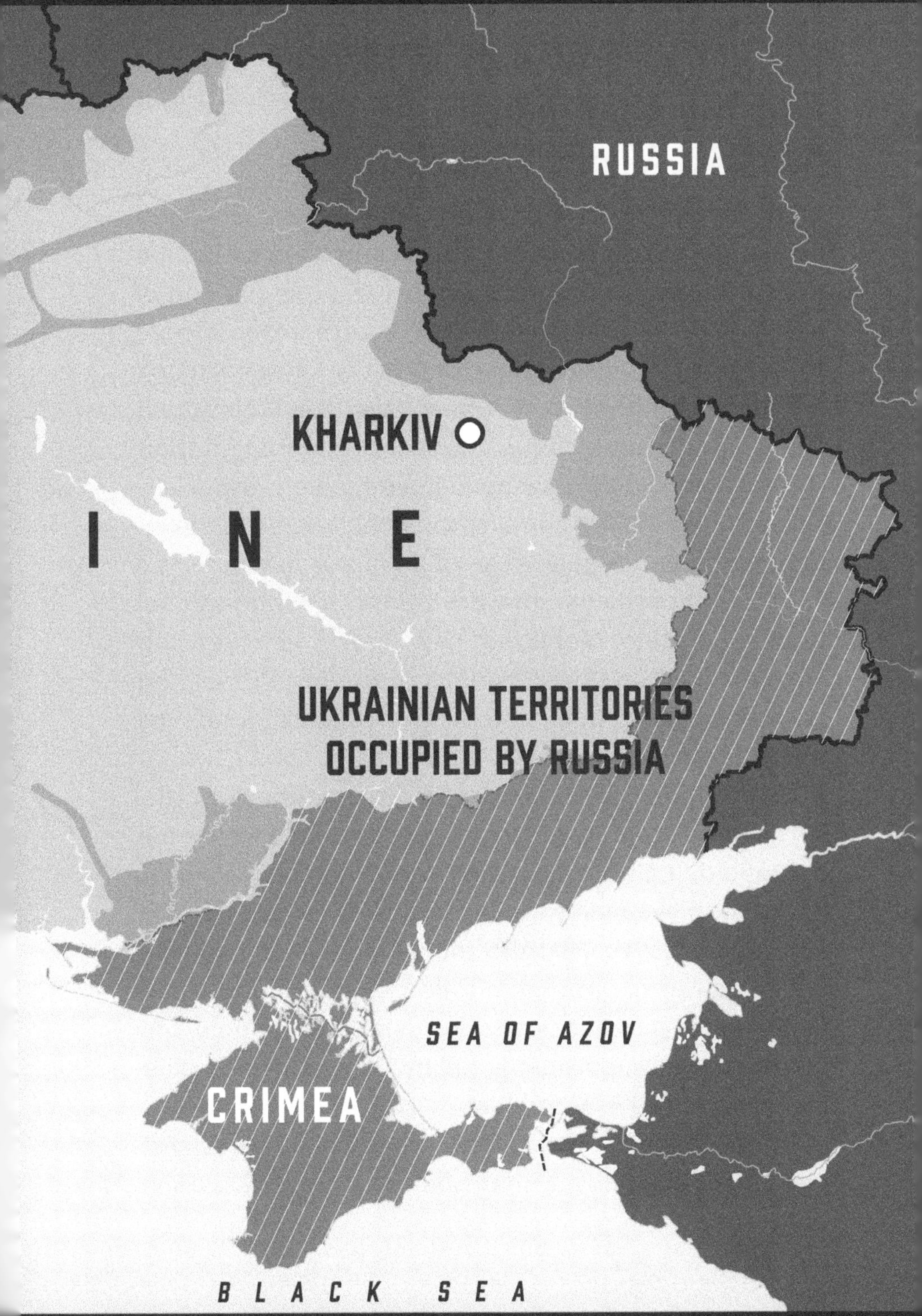
RUSSIA
KHARKIV
I N E
UKRAINIAN TERRITORIES
OCCUPIED BY RUSSIA
SEA OF AZOV
CRIMEA
BLACK SEA

THE NEGATED WAR OF ATTRITION AND THE ADAPTABILITY OF THE RUSSIAN ARMED FORCES

At the beginning of the war, Ukraine achieved a spectacular defensive success. After a few weeks, Ukraine forced Russia to go on the defensive. From the end of March 2022, Russia therefore tried to force trench warfare on Ukraine. The massive use of artillery followed, along with the first introduction of trench warfare. From spring 2022, the war took on the conduct of a war of attrition. The West should have responded adequately, especially since Russia still faced numerous challenges in the reproduction and organization of its forces in the course of 2022. In particular, there were too few operational troops available. Mobilizing new units and increasing arms production posed serious problems; Russia had to "burn" poorly equipped and trained units for months without regard to losses at the front.

Meanwhile, Russia not only overcame these bottlenecks but also improved its military performance on the battlefield. It always found an answer to the high-quality weapon systems supplied by the West (e.g. Javelin anti-tank missiles, HIMARS rocket launchers, AGM-88 anti-radar air-to-ground missiles, Storm Shadow and Scalp cruise missiles, artillery cluster ammunition) and the weapons systems produced by Ukraine itself (including weaponized FPV drones).

The West (or the "Global North") has long underestimated Russia's adaptability on the battlefield and Russia's industrial capabilities—a result of overconfidence and a lack of knowledge about the enemy. In view of the increasing Russian successes and the declining Western support for Ukraine, Russia now senses its opportunity: along the entire almost 1,200 km long front line, increased Russian offensive actions have been clear since the end of 2023. There are also further troop relocations. The Avdiivka area alone has around 40,000 Russian soldiers deployed (out of about 420,000 total deployed Russian soldiers).

The Russian approach has two objectives: on the one hand, to force the Ukrainians to use their tactical and operational reserves; on the other, Russia wants to make local breakthroughs, no matter how small, wherever possible. So they work your way forward step by step stoically and without considering their own losses. The announcement at the end of 2023 that an additional 170,000 Russian soldiers could be added to the armed forces shows Russia's willingness to fight a long war. This means further offensive actions in the medium term. Russian social networks constantly speculate that renewed advances could occur from Russian territory, moving north towards Charkiv, Sumy, or even Chernihiv (north of Kiev). This would significantly extend the 1,200 km long front line for Ukraine and cause even greater fragmentation of the increasingly exhausted Ukrainian forces and resources. Belarusian troops may also be involved.

THE FAILED UKRAINIAN OFFENSIVE AND ITS CONSEQUENCES

The Russians see 2023 as a success. A look at Russian social networks shows this all too well. It is important to consider that Russia suffered one serious setback after another in Ukraine until mid-2022. The most important thing from a Russian perspective: the Russian armed forces repelled the Ukrainian summer offensive in 2023. The deep Russian "Surovikin Line", which was built in over six months from autumn 2022 to spring 2023, has fulfilled its purpose. Further successes include the taking of Bakhmut and Marinka. To uninformed Western observers, Marinka may appear to be just an insignificant town of just under 10,000 people, but with this town the Ukrainian defenders lost another important position that had been built into a fortress for eight years. During the fighting, the city suffered the same fate as Mariupol (May 2022) and Bakhmut (May 2023), with the enemy completely razing it to the ground. At the turn of 2023/24, fierce fighting raged around Avdiivka (fell in February 2024).

The Ukrainians lack the weapons for extensive maneuver warfare. Above all, there is no functioning air force. Nevertheless, by the end of 2022, Ukraine had achieved a few victories—including near Charkiv and Kherson. This is primarily because of US support with reconnaissance data and the Russian problems mentioned. In the Black Sea it was also possible to hit the Russian fleet severely. Until the beginning of June 2023, one could see a tense wait on Russian social networks. This changed suddenly in the summer, after the Russians' first defensive successes against the Ukrainian summer offensive. The Russians' defensive successes masked their high losses. and with images of burning Western Leopard and Challenger tanks, as well as Bradley, Marder and CV-90 armored personnel carriers the mood changed.

Russian forces continued to suffer heavy losses. However, their soldiers are also gaining more and more combat experience. An ongoing analysis of Ukrainian videos of attacks on Russian units clearly shows that they are capable of learning and adapting. The Ukrainians' spectacular defensive successes at certain points cannot hide this fact. Ukrainian soldiers also pay a painful price in blood to gain every piece of knowledge. It is therefore even more worrying that Ukrainian soldiers complain about the lack of combat training in NATO units. This shows that the lessons of the Ukrainian war do not appear to have yet reached the Western armies; There still seems to be a prevailing narrative that Russian soldiers fight in a completely amateur manner. But underestimating your opponent in a fight is the biggest mistake! There could be a nasty surprise there, and Ukrainian officials point this out time and time again.

QUALITY VS. QUANTITY AND THE MISSING EUROPEAN INDUSTRIAL CAPABILITY

The Western weapons systems delivered to Ukraine so far are of high quality, but in a war of attrition it is not quality that is significant, but rather quantity. History has shown often enough: Quality may decide the battle, but the quantity and availability of resources decide the war. Let's take Western anti-aircraft systems as an example. They are making a significant difference at the moment as they are achieving high numbers of kills in the on-going Russian strategic air strikes. But the question is whether Ukraine can maintain these firing rates over the next few months? Especially if the Russians continue to attack—as they did in the first days of the new year—with high quantities of drones, cruise missiles, ballistic missiles and hypersonic weapons. Given the existing Russian precision, every single missile would have to be shot down. A final defensive success is therefore only possible if there is a constant flow of quickly produced anti-aircraft ammunition to Ukraine. At the strategic level, Ukraine currently needs anti-aircraft systems, including ammunition, in order to protect the depths of its space against the second Russian strategic air campaign that is currently underway.

Europe and to some extent the USA have not yet created the conditions that would sustain a war of attrition. It's not just about industrial capacity, but also the associated costs. In this context, it is also about unity, community and, as a result, the attitude towards our–repeatedly in-voked–Western democratic values. What are we willing to sacrifice for this? While the Russians spend manage-able sums to overhaul their combat vehicles and make them combat-ready, equivalent vehicles in the European Union cost many times more. Some experts speak of a cost ratio of 1:40 per combat vehicle. Russia therefore produces not only effectively but also efficiently. Ukraine also suffers from the fact that Russian attacks constantly threaten its already heavily damaged military-industrial complex. She can hardly produce enough of the cheap weapons systems that were quickly available when they were crucial on the battlefield in 2023. Using First Per-son View (FPV) drones stands out here. Their use is currently preventing any deployment and maneuvers on both sides. What barbed wire and machine guns did in the First World War, drones do in the 21st century. They create a "glass battlefield" and thus nip any–especially mechanized–attack in the bud.

THE CURSE AND THE BLESSING OF MODERN WEAPONS SYSTEMS

At the operational level, it would be necessary for Ukraine to target the Russian command structure and logistics through long-range surface-to-surface or air-to-surface weapon systems (e.g. long-range surface-to-surface missiles ATACMS or GLSDB). This would give Ukraine time to reposition itself. Although additional anti-aircraft systems (including a Patriot and IRIS-T system) are arriving, delivery of the GLSDB has been delayed, while ATACMS appear to have only been delivered once. At the tactical level, anti-drone systems (C-UAS) are currently of greatest importance. However, available C-UAS systems are only arriving sparsely the country. These developments are clearly to Ukraine's disadvantage. However, only the warring party that has weapons that help overcome the dilemma described above will be able to take the initiative again. The goal is to control the electromagnetic field. To do this, they are looking for the "miracle weapon" that the commander-in-chief of the Ukrainian armed forces, General Zaluzhnyi, spoke about in his sensational essay "The Fight for the Initiative".

The traditional factors also apply this year: power, space, time and information. Whoever can influence this in their favor with new weapon systems will remain victorious. A positive example should be given at this point for Ukraine: It has defeated the Russian Black Sea Fleet through the use of fast-moving and long-range unmanned surface drone systems (force), based on an "in-time" situation picture (information) provided by the West to push back from the western Black Sea (area) in just a few months. This is a clear success—and it happened so quickly (time) that the Russians still have no real answer to it. Software is increasingly playing a role in supporting target reconnaissance. This is where artificial intelligence comes into play.

Despite these lessons, the capabilities of conventional weapon systems are still very important. The main battle tank, for example, is still the only battlefield weapon that can conquer and seize terrain through high-impact combat. Tanks are highly mobile, have strong armor, and heavy firepower. However, they can only develop their advantages in collaboration. Tanks will always need infantry to support them when necessary—e.g., in urban terrain—in the future it will need mobile short-range anti-aircraft defense (SHORAD or VSHORAD) to protect them against air attack from FPVs or kamikaze drones that are beginning to dominate the battlefield. Dozens of videos of successful FPV attacks on Leopard main battle tanks and Bradley infantry fighting vehicles show this only too well. The Oryx online platform currently lists, among other things, 33 damaged or destroyed Leopard and Challenger main battle tanks as well as 73 damaged or destroyed Bradley, CV90 and Marder armored personnel carriers.

INVISIBLE ALLIES AND SUPPORTERS

Russia could neither fight nor win this war alone. But, and this makes a tremendous difference: It can rely on the "global south" (although this term is also geographically imprecise). Weapons from North Korea and Iran helped the Russians fill shortages. As a result, the Russians were able to continually reinforce and supply their front lines. Through diplomatic initiatives, Russia managed to consolidate its position in the global south and even form new partnerships. New conflicts, such as in the Gaza Strip or the attacks by the Houthis in the Red Sea, are causing increasing problems for the "global north". From the Russian perspective, this is a success and gives the Russian leadership self-confidence. Furthermore, this enables the Russian side to appear correspondingly potent in information warfare, to rally its own population behind it and to continue to attack massively.

The Pope put it well last year when he spoke of a "world war in installments". The current situation is troublesome. Many Western allies are increasingly resigning themselves and are already thinking about a divided Ukraine behind closed doors. At a strategic level, the nuclear armament of both sides—NATO and Russia—means a stalemate, comparable to the situation in the "Cold War" before 1990. The USA continues to be dominant in all types of weapons compared to the main states that threaten it, i.e. China and Russia. However, China in particular poses an increasingly greater challenge for the USA in the maritime area. The USA has this in mind when supporting Ukraine.

NATO also still has powerful air forces available in Europe with corresponding conventional deterrence potential. On the other hand, the state of NATO land forces is critical. Only a few states, such as Poland, for example, have recognized the seriousness of the situation and are massively re-equipping. In the worst case scenario, if Russian troops advanced into the territory of NATO states, NATO would would have to decide to respond by using nuclear weapons to stop them. We can only hope that this does not happen in the medium or long term. Russia meanwhile has a wide range of hybrid options to choose from. These include, among other things: an active "conflict proliferation" and the fomenting of fear in the information space. Putin sees Russia's "historically entitled" borders in the east of NATO–which besides Ukraine, also includes parts of Poland and the Baltic states. The population of these countries naturally sees things differently, as they have had traumatic experiences with Soviet and Russian aggression and occupation in the last century. These states would therefore never give in to a Russian attack–they have learned from their history–but how successfully could they hold out without extensive help from their NATO neighbors?

A MISERABLE WAR WITH INCREASINGLY GLOBAL RAMIFICATIONS

The right of national self-determination applies. It is therefore primarily up to Ukraine to decide how it wants to proceed. At the moment, the clear desire of the majority of the population is to completely liberate the country and become part of the EU and NATO. Historically, we in the West are not aware of the attraction effect that we—the West—triggered in the Central and Eastern European countries after the collapse of the Soviet Union. It was not the USA and Europe that "forced" these countries into the EU and NATO, but rather these countries and their populations that wanted to be part of this community. The "Central Europeans" no longer wanted to be "Eastern Europeans". Consumption and prosperity, i.e. "soft power", were simply too tempting. In a way, this was a repeat of a development that took place in Western Europe after the Second World War—let's remember what a seductive reputation the USA had in the 1950s and 1960s.

Russia could not and cannot offer this. As much as large parts of the Russian population, especially the youth, saw the West as a role model in the 1990s and early 2000s, this was little true for the Russian leadership of the Putin era. On the contrary, an "counter-model" of traditional values was propagated—combined with the patriotic mission to lead Russia back to the greatness it deserves. For a long time, we in the West did not take this danger seriously, thinking, as Francis Fukuyama wrote in 1989, that the "end of history" had arrived. Added to this was the fantasy that major wars were a thing of the past. This wishful thinking has caught up with us, and bit us on the ass.

What do you said to a Ukrainian who said sincerely: "I want to belong to Europe and enjoy the same freedom and prosperity as you!"? Would our selfish response be, "Sorry, we can't do that because then we'd piss off the Russians"? We ourselves secretly wish that everything would be back to normal as quickly as possible. And this is primarily for convenience. So that we can continue to enjoy the prosperity we feel entitled to. A war like this on the fringes of the EU is extremely unpleasant. But we are only of rudimentary interest to the rest of the world—especially "the global south" of the Chinese, Indians, Africans and many others. That is exactly the dilemma, because there is a fear that what we see as the "good old days" are over.

The global world is currently rearranging itself. The "global south", powerfully positioned through technological, economic and demographic developments, is demanding its place. If we compare this with a table at which everyone wants to sit down to eat, i.e. to distribute resources: Up to now we in the West have been very fortunate, but if we are not careful, this will no longer be the case in the future. And we are not prepared for that. Many countries in Europe have remained in a sleeping beauty state for at least a year, if not since the beginning of the conflict—despite all the lip service paid to them. It is up to us to make the difference—in our own interest.

The article appeared in "SIRIUS. Journal for strategic analyses", issue 1/2024. Reprinted with kind permission of the editors and publisher de Gruyter.

www.degruyter.com/journal/key/sirius/html

MARKUS REISNER

Colonel in the General Staff Service, officer in the Austrian Armed Forces, doctorate in history and PhD in law at the University of Vienna; repeated assignments abroad in Bosnia and Herzegovina, Kosovo, Afghanistan, Iraq, Chad, Central Africa and Mali. Research focus: Use and future of unmanned reconnaissance and weapon systems, historical and current military topics. Currently Commander of the Guards of the Austrian Armed Forces.

The Russian attack on Ukraine on the morning of February 24, 2022 initially ended in a debacle for the aggressor. Nonetheless, the Russians have adapted to the consistently changing conditions.

STRATEGIC FACTORS
LEADERSHIP

1

U p to the writing of this work, the perspective of Russian operations divides the war in Ukraine into four phases. First, the armed forces of the Russian Federation tried to crush Ukraine through a rapid advance. There was an attack by an army of 200,000 men in five force groupings on a broad front along the entire Ukrainian-Russian and parts of the Ukrainian-Belarusian border. Central attack axes were already apparent early on in the Donbass, on the Black Sea coast and north of Kiev. However, the Russian side did not choose a clearly recognizable focus, as they brought together comparable forces for all attack movements.

Today we know that each military district was responsible for a line of advance and prepared the forces for it from its area of responsibility. Each Russian brigade set up one or two battalion tactical groups (BTG), which were capable of independent combined arms combat for a limited period of time. This means close cooperation between armored troops, artillery, engineers, logistics and other troops. However, combined combat at the battalion level is a relatively new development in the Russian armed forces, which is due to the glaring weaknesses of the previously common division and brigade structures. These proved to be no longer up to date in the 2008 campaign against Georgia. The subsequent restructuring of the Russian army contributed significantly to the fact that practically all experts in the West supposedly recognized a significant increase in quality and consequently gave Ukraine very little chance when the invasion began. However, in the early weeks of the war, this reformed force failed in northern Ukraine and was unable to quickly break through to and take the capital. It is worth a closer analysis of the Russian force approach.

We are unsure if the Russian structure still maintains the Battalion Tactical Group (BTG), or if it will be replaced by some other type of structure. However, it is very likely that they abandoned this structure after the first weeks of the war. Initially it consisted of a proportion of combat troops, usually with a tank company and two armoured or motorized infantry companies. There was also a comparatively strong artillery component, each with a battery of rocket and tube artillery, as well as the so-called breakthrough artillery. These are TOS-1 launchers for thermobaric rockets, which fire at a comparatively short distance of three to four kilometers immediately before the combat troops attack the break-in site. The BTG also has both a ground-based reconnaissance platoon and drones. Other combat support forces included electronic warfare units to disrupt enemy communications, as well as engineer and anti-aircraft forces. In addition, there was the operational support from medical and logistics elements. There were at least twelve different skills available, all of which had to be used correctly in the field by the BTG commander. However, in the Russian armed forces, tactical decisions on the ground are not made with the same planning effort as at higher levels. Therefore, the command staff of these combat groups is very small. However, in order to be able to conduct the battle quickly and successfully, such a staff must be organized according to the division of labor. As a result, it automatically grows to a certain minimum size, which was probably not the case here. This also explains the relatively slow attack speed of the units, even under favorable conditions.

The widespread view in the Western media that Russian officers are simply too stupid to carry out quick attacks is not only wrong, but also very dangerous. Under the given conditions, the vast majority of Western commanders would probably fail. Markus Reisner, Colonel in the Austrian Armed Forces, writes about the leadership of the BTGs:

At the tactical level, lengthy planning is not done. From a Western perspective, Russian tactical-level commanders have limited opportunities to develop plans for specific tasks. Rather, they choose from a "menu" of known "tactics" in response to certain military situation developments—an approach that, in the Austrian understanding, corresponds more closely to combat

"On February 25, 2022, I joined a real people's army. People from all walks of life serve there. [...] 'Good businessmen are also good commanders' is an expression I have heard three times: first in Donetsk Oblast from a battalion commander, then near Zaporizhzhia from the leader of a reconnaissance platoon, and then near Kharkiv from a man wearing the number 88 Forbes list of the richest Ukrainians. All three were successful businessmen before the war and all three are good commanders now."

Pavlo Kazarin, Ukrainian volunteer in an interview in February 2023 *technology (as at the company level). The commander therefore applies standard combat procedures at the BTG mass level.*

In this respect, the reform of the Russian army brought about a structural change based on the Western model, but it did not implement any decisive changes in the training and leadership orientation. However, in order to lead such a structure in combat successfully, this would have been absolutely necessary. Ukrainian striking power resulted less in the high Russian losses of armored vehicles in the first year of the war less than did the significant lack of leadership on the Russian side.

Up to April 2023, the fighting could be divided into four phases. In the first phase until the beginning of April 2022, a rapid advance by strong armored troops in the Kiev area failed, while the attacks on the Black Sea coast and in Donbas were comparatively successful, but have been much slower than expected.

In April and May 2022, the Russian BTGs adjusted their tactics and attempted to keep their own casualties low through massive artillery fire with support from higher levels. However, the same weaknesses emerged again, especially in the battle for Engen, such as the attempted bridge attacks near Donetsk. The scope of the operations had to be significantly reduced from June onwards due to heavy losses and the beginning of mobilization in Russia. The Ukrainian General Staff recognized this short window of relative weakness and launched a counteroffensive in the fall that was considerable considering Ukraine's material and personnel capabilities.

With the onset of winter at the end of 2022 until this work was written, the fighting along the entire front developed into a modern trench warfare in which both sides wear each other out with high losses, especially in the infantry fight for urban areas and field fortifications. The Ukrainian summer offensive in 2023 didn't change anything about that. At none of these times was it expected that Russian BTGs could achieve a real breakthrough and operations in deep space, since their command staff, the planning capacity of the tiny staffs and the logistics structure were not at all designed for this. The first armored combat groups were deployed on the German side in the Second World War and since then it has been clear that the logistical supply of such units, especially during an attack, is an immense challenge. Due to its victory in WWII, the Red Army and Soviet political leadership held on to the practice of only providing superior resources at the operational level. Tactical flexibility and sophistication were never encouraged or nurtured to become operational factors. Soviet thinking was that if this approach defeated the German Wehrmacht then it must be the right way to do things. They also considered the unchanged use of the BTGs as logical in the 21st Century, based on the Russian Army's success with this approach in 2014 and the proven effectiveness of these structures in Syria— albeit against a much weaker opponent. However, this approach immediately faltered when it came up against a well-trained, adequately equipped and determined opponent like Ukraine in February 2022. So, to what extent has the Russian leadership adapted to the realities of the war in Ukraine?

Over the winter of 2022/23, the Russian armed forces shortened the front line to the extent possible and prepared formations for new offensive operations. We may assume that they also restructured their approach and implemented operational training measures. In any case, the attacks by the Russian army in the first months of 2023 were carried out on a much smaller scale. Essentially, mixed assault companies were used during this period. This seemingly new approach is actually an integral part of old Soviet doctrine and is arguably still being developed. These units have a comparatively low infantry strength, a mixed armored platoon of infantry fighting vehicles and main battle tanks, their own fire support such as tubular artillery and mortars, as well as reconnaissance and medical forces. This kit is used to form a single assault platoon adapted to the mission, which is then supposed to defeat the enemy's field fortifications and other pockets of resistance with the support of the remaining company components. While in Western armed forces such a shock force can quickly grow to 40 men or more, the core of the Russian equivalent consists of four squads (Russian: troika) of three men each. Another machine gun squad, mortar team, sharp shooters, flamethrowers and/or medics can reinforce this officer-led group. Often the number of operational IFVs (maximum four in the company) will determine the size of the element. Furthermore, together with one or two main battle tanks, they provide direct fire support at the start of the attack. Since there are no real group structures and the forms of cooperation change daily or even hourly, the internal cohesion of these sub-units, especially when allocating the regularly necessary replacement fields, can be assessed as at least questionable. The lack of a qualified non-commissioned officer corps in the Russian army has a particular impact here—a deficiency that the Ukrainian army has largely overcome with Western training support. When attacking Ukrainian trenches, Russian officers are not only confronted with a difficult combat task, but also have to compensate for structural problems.

Let's place ourselves in the shoes of the Russian attacker: Let's consider a scenario where a Russian assault company is fully manned and equipped with all the necessary weapon systems, ammunition, and supplies. The Russian shock troop leader is now given the combat task of taking a Ukrainian trench in his sector of the front. He usually has less than a day to prepare because his superiors are under pressure to be able to demonstrate success. He makes the best possible use of this time to use drones to investigate the relevant area and possible break-through points. Once he has made a decision, he marshals his forces. Four BMP-2 armored personnel carriers can bring its forces up to about 150 meters in front of the enemy position. Each vehicle can transport up to seven men, resulting in a dismounted strength of 28 men—which is not even a regular infantry platoon strength in the West. In addition to his lead squad (himself, a radio operator and a drone operator), he takes with him his three original squads of three men each: a machine gun squad, a bazooka squad and a rifle squad with a medic. There are still 16 places left. He decides on another machine gun squad (three men), a flamethrower squad (six men), a light mortar squad (three men) and a medical squad (four men). With these powers he can fire and move independently and always has a machine gun in every element. It also has an immediate component for indirect fire (mortars) and direct entry into the trenches (flame throwers). Furthermore, he does not have to use the medical squad to withdraw infantrymen to rescue the wounded, which he will certainly have in an attack on a fortified position. In addition, he has artillery support and fire from main battle tanks and armored personnel carriers at his disposal.

All the necessary elements are supposedly in place to make a breakthrough against a group of entrenched Ukrainians armed with a machine gun. However, due to the very high personnel turnover due to high losses, and the lack of subordinate commanders, he has to lead almost all elements himself and directly. In our case he has to command no less than seven squad leaders and two men in his own squad. In addition, he has to maintain a constant overview and assessment of the combat situation, stay in radio contact with his superiors, and coordinate fire support and care of the wounded.

Such a structure pushes even the best leaders to their limits. It is generally believed that almost anyone can learn to manage three elements, or up to five with talent or training. Only really, really good leaders with

"The fight is here. I need ammunition, not a taxi."

Volodymyr Zelensky, President of Ukraine,
in an unconfirmed telephone conversation with
the US administration regarding an evacuation
offer on February 24, 2022

experience in the field can work with seven. This explains why real successes have only been achieved sporadically: the Russian army certainly has some military talents that can have a positive impact under favorable conditions. Now, one could argue that our young Russian lieutenant could also go into battle with a less complex structure. However, if you want to attack a field fortification with determined defenders, and are able to take more people and more firepower, then you will. The sometimes frivolous statements in the media regularly ignore the realities of armed confrontations: it is easy to be an armchair strategist. Despite all the limitations, the Russian armed forces have managed to take over sections of terrain slowly but surely through countless of these assault attacks with very limited targets—for example in the Bakhmut area.

It currently seems questionable whether the Russian army can compensate for its glaring leadership deficits at all levels through numerical superiority alone. All the tactical adjustments that have been observed so far seem to indicate that Russian officers are stuck in their traditional thinking patterns and will likely remain so for the course of the war.

More astonishing, is the enormous progress that the Ukrainian Army has made since its catastrophic combat performance of 2014 and 2015. After all, both armies and therefore all senior, older officers come from Soviet times. But the Ukrainians quickly learned that only armed forces with a distinctly decentralized leadership structure can survive such a comprehensive and far-reaching attack.

This means that soldiers at the front line and at a low rank level can use their initiative and make crucial, on-the-spot tactical decisions.

This principle is called 'mission command'. In contrast to a rigid command structure in which platoons, companies and battalions only act when they are told what to do, when to do it, and where to do it, with mission command there is always scope to take the initiative yourself or even to act contrary to previous orders, because the situation at your front has changed. Because of extensive Western training in recent years, it is little surprise that the Ukrainian infantry and special forces have been able to operate like this. What is truly astonishing, however, is that this complete change in mindset appears to be widespread in the National Guard, Territorial Forces, and Reserves as well. However, we should not underestimate the significance of this sea change, as changing the fundamental mindset of soldiers is much more challenging than simply training them to specific content.

"We have a different style and this Ukrainian way is quite consistent with Western doctrine: leaders have the freedom to adapt and can achieve their goals in accordance with the assessment of the situation on the ground. In practice, the Soviet model means simply following exact written orders from a commander."

Mykhailo Samus, former Ukrainian officer,
head of the Ukrainian think-tank
New Geopolitics Research Network.

In addition to drones, loitering ammunition represents a special challenge in the new battlefield. The Russian 'Lancet' is used like a kind of kamikaze drone with pinpoint precision against artillery, tanks and other targets.

WEAPONS TECHNOLOGY

Drones have become an incredibly important weapon thanks to the war in Ukraine. This conflict is neither the first war in which drones have been used, nor the first in which both sides use this tool. But never has such a large amount been utilized for military purposes. The Ukrainian armed forces are currently using around 10,000 drones per month, signifying a new dimension in their importance. In fact, both sides have announced enormous increases in drone production for the war year 2024. The tremendous variety of types is also new. The proliferation of small, inexpensive drones is particularly affecting options on the battlefield. Initially used primarily as a means of reconnaissance, small commercial drones are now also a crucial means of effectiveness thanks to the mass use of FPV (First Person View) drones as of 2023.

These numbers are significant because drones are capable of taking on all other missions previously carried out by the expensive manned aircraft of regular air forces: reconnaissance and surveillance, close air support, precision strikes against high-value targets, and so on.

All areas of military use are now being rethought and examined to determine the extent to which drones can have an impact across all dimensions (land, air, sea).

The innovative wide-spread use of weaponized commercial UAVs (Unmanned Aerial Vehicles) that only cost a few thousand, or even hundreds of Euros, has given cause for concern beyond of the War in Ukraine though. The same approach used by the Ukrainians against the Russian Army could also be used by terrorists against civilians elsewhere. So authorities around the world are looking at what actions they need to take in order to prevent the next 9/11 being committed with drones.

The true consequences of the tactical movement of massed forces on the digital battlefield are also unfolding before our eyes. The constant threat of detection through persistent aerial reconnaissance means, above all, that camouflage discipline is increasingly relevant for forces on the ground. This initially includes classic camouflage, in which soldiers and equipment merge as completely as possible with their surroundings using optical illusions. But that alone is not enough. Taking camouflage into account is important in operational planning as it influences troop behavior. The objective is to decrease all signature factors, including movement, heat, light, and noise. While it has always been the case, it's now more challenging to go unnoticed when breaking camouflage guidelines because of the current conditions. Part of the answer to the question of how to defend against the "new" threat posed by unmanned systems is an age-old one: iron discipline. By combining this important core capability with new, signature-reducing technologies, we can decrease the effectiveness of the currently omnipresent reconnaissance drones.

Aside from unmanned systems, most of the technologies used in the war in Ukraine since 2022 are not new. Even the latest battle tanks and self-propelled howitzers are children of the 1980s. Javelin missiles have been around since the mid-1990s, and even the much-noticed ATACMS missiles were first ready for series production just as the Berlin Wall was falling. Many of these systems are so old that spare parts or suitable ammunition are no longer produced for them. Ironically however, some of these weapons are being used in combat for the first time in Ukraine—which is of great interest to those countries that have these weapons in their arsenals.

What applies to older systems is doubly important for new technology: the data sets that are generated every day on the battlefronts of this war are probably the most valuable information that currently exists for the armaments sector worldwide. So far, the Ukrainian leadership has proven adept at providing relevant data to Western nations and manufacturers in return for Western arms supplies. NATO also has an opportunity to take a closer look at the entire spectrum of Russian armaments thanks to the Ukraine War. However, this information windfall also applies to the other side as well. For example, the Russian Federation exhibited Western weapons captured in Ukraine during its "Army 2023" military exhibition—including equipment such as the Swedish-made CV-90 armored personnel carrier.

But how do you judge whether a particular weapon has had a great or decisive influence on the war, or has even maybe not proven that useful at all? To understand this, we must analyze what effect the system was able to generate and at what price. In addition, the question "What if?" seems very hypothetical but needs to be considered realistically.

For our purposes, we selected the examples below because each of these weapons has received a lot of coverage in the media—which has in turn given some of them an almost mythological reputation.

▶ EXAMPLE A [UKR]: "JAVELIN" ANTI-TANK MISSILE

The Javelin is a portable anti-tank handgun that weighs just over 22 kilograms when ready to fire. The missile has automatic infrared homing, enabling the shooter to fire the weapon and immediately change position (fire-and-forget) without the requirement of actively steering it towards the target. The rocket hits armored vehicles in the so-called top attack mode, which means it first gains altitude and then hits the enemy tank from above into the thinner roof armor. The current model has a range of up to 2.5 kilometers and can overcome additional armor thanks to its tandem warhead with two charges one behind the other. The Javelin is a weapon system that the Ukrainian army received well before the start of the invasion in February 2022. NATO swiftly supplied additional deliveries to the existing weapons, enabling Ukraine to have over 8,000 launchers that only required missile installation. Training on the Javelin is also relatively easy and quick to carry out. The longer range and top attack mode make the Javelin even more versatile than simpler anti-tank hand weapons, such as the Panzerfaust 3 or NLAW, which were also delivered. However, the users require vehicle support, as dismounted forces can carry the large missiles only a shorter distance.

When the Russian battalion combat groups first moved across the border, a very dynamic situation without a rigid front line arose along the entire border–particularly in the north. By utilizing both planned and impromptu tactics, Ukrainian infantry units turned the tables on the ill-prepared enemy and lured them into deadly ambushes that gained global recognition. The Javelin is ideal for these situations as it has a high probability of successfully hitting from a long distance, and allows users to withdraw immediately after firing and move to a new position to attack again from a different location. Based on previous combat experience and the data available to date, we can calculate that the Ukrainian infantrymen achieved a hit rate of at least 80% during this initial phase of the war. Since each missile costs about $240,000, and the CLU (Command Launch Unit) is reused, each combat operation incurred a cost of just over $300,000. If the target was a Russian T-80 BVM main battle tank, which costs at least $3 million to become operational, we can calculate that the Javelin is a hugely cost-effective solution. Even lightly armored vehicles like the BTR-80 cost well over $500,000 to produce, so the Javelin was an excellent means of grinding down the enemy in this phase of the war.

In addition, the logistical footprint of the weapon system is minimal, as only the missiles need to be re-supplied to the front and there is no need for complex training facilities. This combination of rapid availability, good performance parameters, favorable cost efficiency, and the tactically appropriate situation make it possible to say that the Javelin, along with other anti-tank hand weapons, constituted a decisive weapon system for the first weeks of the war. The stylization of "Saint Javelin, the protector of Ukraine" that became very popular on social media definitely had justification.

However, the situation was different as the war pro-gressed: with the solidification of the fronts and the tran-sition to trench warfare, situations in which ambushes could be staged to block enemy movements no longer existed. In this tactical environment, the Javelin was used less, or was used to take out other, stationary targets. Since both sides now expose their armored vehicles less during attacks, there were also fewer high-value targets.

Infantry forces now fought in field fortifications and buildings, against targets and equipment that only costs a few thousand Euros. So if you take out a machine-gun costing a few thousand Euros with a Javelin that costs $240,000 USD per shot, this is no longer a cost-effective way to win the battle. However, if its deployment also saves friendly lives, it can still make sense, especially given Ukraine's more limited reserves of manpower.

At any rate, the Javelin is no longer such a crucial weapon system for Ukraine. So the question "What if?" The effectiveness of Western anti-tank weapons like the Javelin in the first weeks of the war raises serious questions about whether the invaders' armored combat troops could have been stopped without them.

▶ EXAMPLE B (RUS): BMP-T "TERMINATOR"

The BMP-T is neither a main battle vehicle nor an infantry fighting vehicle. Rather, it is a fire support vehicle that is intended to supplement the limited effectiveness of battle tanks in urban terrain and thereby reduce their vulnerability. The origins of this concept lie in the Russian experience of the first Chechen war, in which there were massive losses of armored vehicles in Grozny due to simple hand held anti-tank weapons. The BMP-T consists of a T-72 chassis with a remotely controlled, but thinly armored turret, that is equipped with various weapons, including: four launch tubes for anti-tank guided missiles, two 30mm machine cannons, two grenade launchers, and a PKM machine gun.

Since its introduction in 2002, only a small double-digit number of the vehicle has been produced so far. Analysts believe that its first deployment in Ukraine occurred during the battle for the cities of Sievierodonetsk and Lysychansk in May and June 2022. Based on the rare sightings, even in Russian media, analysts assume that the Russian Army has never deployed more than a dozen BMP-Ts to the front at any time. Also, as of now, we know that at least five of these vehicles have been destroyed, and another three have suffered damage of an unknown degree. For years, Russian state television praised the BMP-T as a miracle weapon, and its deployment in Ukraine received broad media coverage. But even if the vehicle were to fulfill all its promises, the small number of them deployed ensures that these vehicles cannot have a decisive impact under any circumstances. Moreover, since there have been enormous losses of Russian tanks in Ukraine—particularly in urban battles where the "Terminator" was supposed to be in its prime—it is extremely doubtful that the BMP-T has even come close to fulfilling its purpose. If we compare this negligible benefit with the huge development and manufacturing costs of this vehicle, the result shows an extremely poor cost-benefit ratio. How would the conflict have gone so far without the BMP-T? There probably wouldn't be any noticeable difference—other than a few less destroyed Russian armored vehicles.

▶ EXAMPLE C (UKR): ANTI-AIRCRAFT TANK "GEPARD" (CHEETAH)

The Gepard anti-aircraft tank first entered production in the early 1970s, and was intended to protect armored combat troops from fighter aircraft and helicopters. The Gepard is a powerful air defense system with two cannons that can rapidly fire 35mm rounds. These cannons are controlled by an on-board radar system and can effectively target and engage threats within a range of up to 5.5 kilometers.

In the summer of 2022, Ukraine received the first Gepard to protect important facilities and equipment from the Russian air threat. Since the weapon system has been out of production for a long time, and has never been used in combat before, there were only small quantities of its ammunition available. Some international stocks of the ammunition also faced usability issues because of a lack of compatibility (as with Norway) or export restrictions (as with Switzerland). This shortage of ammunition hindered the Gepard's readiness for action. There were similar problems with the supply of spare parts, and it was unclear to what extent Ukraine's future needs could be met.

Despite any misgivings, the Gepard proved to be a very robust and effective system in combat, with a high success rate. To secure the supply of ammunition, Rheinmetall also quickly set up a completely new production facility in record time and is already delivering fresh supplies of ammunition to Ukraine. The Gepard's rapid-fire cannons were particularly effective in combating Iranian Shahed drones, which are being used in large numbers by the Russians. In at least one case, a Gepard crew also shot down a Russian Kh-101 cruise missile.

Even though the Shahed drones only cost $20-60,000 each, depending on the version, the cost of the five or six 35mm shells needed to shoot one down with a Gepard is much lower. Also, as the Gepard poses a threat to the regular Russian air force as well, it delivers a positive impact simply by its presence. Therefore, it is an extremely cost-effective weapon system. However, as there are no plans to restart production of Gepards, each one is precious, and the inability to replace or refurbish destroyed or damaged systems limits their overall operational value.

Nevertheless, it is worth noting that the Gepard, alongside powerful but much more expensive missile defense systems such as IRIS-T, plays a crucial role in Ukraine's air defense. What if Ukraine had never received the Gepard? Russian aircraft would have had greater operational freedom—causing more casualties and destruction—and potentially leading to a decisive outcome.

▶ EXAMPLE D (RUS): "LANCET" LOITERING MUNITION

The first deployment of Russian Lancet drones occurred in Syria in 2020. These drones are now offered in three different versions: Lancet-1, Lancet-3 (slightly larger), and the new, more powerful Izdeliye-53 and the latest variant, Izdeliye-55. According to Zala Aero, the Izdeliye-55, unveiled in September 2023, is resistant to electronic countermeasures. However, this scenario is highly improbable because the drone's data transmission capabilities would be susceptible to ECM disruption.

So far, the Lancet-3 model has seen the most widespread use in Ukraine. The Lancet-3 has a maximum payload capacity of only three kilograms (normally a high explosive charge) and can fly for approximately 40 minutes. Lancet can loiter of a designated area, up to its maximum flight time, and engage emerging targets under user control. According to Russian sources, a complete system costs around $35,000, but multiple systems are needed in order to monitor a target area most effectively. Although the Lancet-3 uses Western technologies from nVidia and AMD, the Russian defense industry can increase production to probably several hundred units per month.

Lancet's confirmed "kills" include 11 main battle tanks, 24 artillery pieces, plus a MiG-29 and SU-25 aircraft. The actual numbers are probably far higher, as these are only unequivocal confirmations with images from at least two different sources.

Radar-controlled anti-aircraft guns have proven to be the only effective weapons against the Lancet, but these systems, such as the Gepard, are no longer in widespread use and must also be in the right place at the right time because their effective range is relatively short. The extensive use of the Lancet on the front lines poses a growing problem for the Ukrainians, as the Russian military-industrial complex is increasing production of these systems. So, despite the system's low lethality, Lancet-3 can be a very cost-effective weapon—particularly against Ukraine's limited number of artillery systems.

The Lancet-3's potential effectiveness against Ukrainian fighter aircraft in the deeper battlespace is noteworthy and sheds light on the current state of Russian artillery. Using the Lancet-3 to attack a mobile high-value target over a long distance is much more complex than using precise rocket artillery to destroy it. But unlike complex artillery systems, the production of Lancets is easier because they can be manufactured using simpler methods. Russian companies can ensure production by obtaining western civilian electronics through China, bypassing western sanctions.

What would the war look like without Lancet? As I write this, the lingering lingering ammunition supply has unquestionably altered the tactical behavior of the Ukrainian armed forces and poses a significant peril. The combination of reconnaissance and FPV drones, as well as loitering ammunition, enables a chain of effects without endangering friendly forces at the front. In some areas of application, the Russian army has also compensated for its lack of precision artillery by using the Lancet-3. The Russian army has also strategically impacted the West by acquiring technologies for use in the Lancet-3 and other models—despite embargoes and sanctions.

▶ EXAMPLE E (UKR): MARITIME CRUISE MISSILES / UNMANNED SURFACE SYSTEMS

The Russian Black Sea Fleet has always outmatched Ukraine in terms of classic naval weapon systems. However, as of 2021, a Ukrainian cruise missile, R-360 "Neptune", developed from the Soviet Kh-35, became operational. These missiles destroyed the Russian cruiser Moskva and a Russian Kilo-class submarine, causing the Russian Federation's largest single-incident losses of the war to-date.

Neptune is currently undergoing modifications to incorporate a guidance system that will enable it to engage both naval and land targets. While the exact cost of this cruise missile is unknown, it is likely a highly cost-effective way of destroying large, complex surface warships.

In terms of cost-effectiveness, however, the new sea drones surpass any cruise missile. These simple, unmanned, remote-controlled vessels carry up to 300 kilograms of explosives to their target at high speed. Several units of the Russian Navy, as well as port facilities and important infrastructure, such as bridges, have already been severely affected. There is virtually no effective defensive armament in the Russian inventory that provides protection against these small, fast vessels either. By utilizing shore-based/launched cruise missiles and drones, Ukraine has effectively expelled the Russian Black Sea Fleet from the Black Sea. The strategic impact of this combination of abilities is clear, as the sea route is now accessible to Ukraine once more. This in turn has made sea-based commando operations possible for Ukrainian special forces, further weakening critical infrastructure in Crimea such as Russia's air defense systems. As a result, Ukraine can more readily deploy its military assets in the Black Sea region. Larger-scale amphibious landing operations against Russian assets in Crimea are also certainly conceivable in the future, as Ukrainian marines have passed through complete training by the British Royal Marines.

▶ EXAMPLE F: "COPE CAGES" VS. FPV-DRONES

In Iraq and Afghanistan, many Coalition vehicles were upgraded with cage armor to safeguard against RPG-7 and similar anti-tank hand weapons. As of November 2021, Russian main battle tanks have undergone installation of cage armor, also known as slat armor, on their roofs. The aim was to improve protection against 'top-attack' anti-tank missiles like the Javelin. Despite the mass distribution of this improvisation, Western missiles were not hindered by it at all and continued to reliably destroy Russian tanks. The term "cope cage" that emerged on social media and then became world famous was primarily used to make fun of the poor performance of the Russian armed forces.

However, the widespread use of so-called FPV drones (First Person View), i.e. powerful and inexpensive drones that can be flown into even the smallest targets, such as tank hatches, has made cage armor relevant again for both sides. Fighting positions and armored vehicles are now protected by improvised structures made of metal and wood. These 'cages' also offer a certain level of protection against improvised drone bombers and loitering munitions. While people laughed at these countermeasures at the beginning of the war, they have now become a necessary part of everyday life at the front, and have as much of a decisive impact as camouflage measures.

"The moment a target enters our surveillance area, we are given a battle order. Next, we swiftly relocate to a clear firing position for optimal radar functionality. Near Odessa, our crew managed to shoot down ten Shahed drones in just one engagement. Destroying the target only requires three shots from each barrel. This is the perfect weapon to use against drones."

"Mars", a member of a Ukrainian unit equipped with the Gepard anti-aircraft tank in December 2022

"Electronic warfare is the key to victory in drone warfare."

General Valerii Zaluzhnyi, Commander-in-Chief of the Ukrainian Armed Forces

"I don't need reinforcements. I need buildings to fight from!"

Radio message from a Ukrainian battalion commander about the extent of the destruction in the Battle of Severodonetsk

"Whoever can limit the enemy's precision effectiveness through electronic warfare will win this war."

Colonel Ivan Pavlenko, commander of the combat support troops of the Ukrainian Armed Forces

Retired from the Bundeswehr's inventory in Germany, the Gepard anti-aircraft tank has experienced a great resurgence in the Ukraine. This shows how powerful this weapon system still is—even in the fight against drones.

3
TRAINING

I n 2014, the Ukrainian military displayed significant shortcomings in all areas during the Russian invasion and annexation of Crimea and were completely unprepared for the conflict that ensued. Therefore, fundamental reforms were necessary across all military structures in Ukraine. Even if the Russian armed forces' operational plan for the full invasion of Ukraine had clear weaknesses, it was still a full-scale attack along the country's border that had to be blocked and/or repelled. Despite this, the international perception was that the Ukrainian army was weaker than the Russian army. And yet the Ukrainian army did successfully block the Russian advance. How was this possible? The apparent success of the Ukrainian army's comprehensive modernization is remarkable. In the past seven years, the Ukrainians have made a systemic change that is unlike anything seen in recent military history.

The use of modern technologies such as Western anti-tank missiles, drones, etc. has certainly contributed to the Ukrainian's success. However, in order to use such resources successfully, realistic and relevant training is required. Since 2014, Ukrainian combat troops have received significant training support from NATO forces, particularly Anglo-American special forces.

The initial deliveries from NATO countries immediately after the start of the invasion consisted primarily of material with little or no training requirement (such as the Panzerfaust 3, or stocks of former Warsaw Pact weaponry that the Ukrainians were already familiar with). However, over time, the systems delivered became more complex, and meanwhile, the Ukrainians needed to maintain a wide range of capabilities, covering everything from small arms to sophisticated rocket artillery systems and combat aircraft.

However, Ukraine lacked the comprehensive training infrastructure to cover all of these systems and platforms, which is why tens of thousands of Ukrainian soldiers were trained in NATO countries. There was initial skepticism among Western trainers whether the Ukrainians could achieve sufficient operational readiness in such a short time. But NATO trainers now find themselves in situations where Ukrainian soldiers criticize some of the alliance's training methods as being outdated. You don't need insider knowledge to realize that some of these courses certainly lack relevance to the current combat reality in Ukraine.

There is currently a significant disparity in resources: the Ukrainian armed forces have valuable combat experience and vast data sets to go with it. NATO, on the other hand, can produce and supply sophisticated military equipment. The performance data and capability profiles of Western military technology regularly impressed frontline fighters. While most of the systems are proving their worth in combat, it is in training where there is a significant need for change in NATO. This was already foreseeable well before 2022.

Moreover, the deliveries from the different inventories of the mixed equipment from European armies have also produced a wide variety of equipment types in the Ukrainian inventory, which understandably complicates logistics and readiness. Standardization is being sought but can only be achieved if manufacturers in Western countries drastically increase their production capacity and speed. In addition, Ukraine's leadership is pushing the development of its own armaments sector to become more self-sufficient. However, for the supply large-scale equipment, this will still take some time. It is unclear whether the development of relevant weapons systems is even possible—given the constant Russian threat from the air and cyberspace, as well as the shortage of skilled workers because of military service and casualties.

On the Russian side, it is currently almost impossible to gain insight into their training organizations and methods. However, applied and observed operational experience shows that the Russian Army provides only rudimentary combat training. The lower management level in particular shows glaring weaknesses, which leads to significant losses of personnel and material, and can be a sign of too little training time and/or misguided content. However, in the course of the war so far, various Russian units have shown a certain ability to learn. Changes in combat technology and tactics usually appeared at the same time on several sectors of the front. Therefore, we can assume that either central authorities order such modifications from above or that newly mobilized units receive modified training.

Both warring parties currently face the classic dilemma of having to create well-trained fighting units, while also needing to replace losses at the front with new soldiers. This requires skilled trainers, who are all too often need-

"The helicopters fired volleys of unguided rockets to hold down Russian firing positions. As soon as we were close enough, we also fired machine guns at everything we could see. We flew with open ramps to get to the ground quicker. As soon as we were deep enough, everyone jumped out. We entered the first building from two sides, my group on the left and the "Neptune" group on the right. We covered each other. The enemy was entrenched in the village on the other side of the island, and the buildings in the landing zone were completely destroyed by our artillery and air strikes. We had wounded and killed, and the resistance was fierce."

"Skin", group leader of the anti-terrorist unit Alpha on the Ukrainian landing attempt on Snake Island.

ed as leaders in combat. Thanks to comprehensive support from the West, Ukraine is currently probably better positioned to achieve the combination of relevance and time efficiency required in this context. However, it raises questions about the extent to which Ukraine can use the methods and means of the Western concept of mobile warfare. While it is at least clear that today's Russia is no longer prepared for the resource-intensive combat doctrine of the Soviet era, the structures and mindsets of NATO's land forces also need a comprehensive review to remain current on the battlefields of Ukraine. Depending on the NATO country concerned, this has only happened to a limited extent or not at all so far.

Currently, we cannot estimate the extent to which the Russian defense industry can compensate for losses and provide more modern systems without technological support from the West. In the war year of 2023, there were numerous indications of serious problems, especially in the areas of armored vehicles and ammunition production. The front-line deployment of small numbers of new armored vehicles such as the BMP-3 or the T-90 suggests that ongoing production is at a small scale that can only partially compensate for losses at the front. The large number of increasingly older systems at the front (e.g. T-54 and BMP-1) suggests that the Russian defense sector is finding it easier to make stored vehicles ready for combat than to increase production of newer models.

From 2014 to 2015, Ukraine relied on local militias to defend itself, some of which had sporadic neo-fascist leanings. Ultimately, however, these irregular forces countered Russian influence when the Ukrainian army could not do so. It is primarily because of this fact that some of these associations still exist today. However, since the comprehensive invasion in 2022, the regular forces, now significantly more powerful, have also assumed the moral function of the early militia movements, leading to the observation of a real national mobilization that affects all areas of society since then. Since 2022, crowdfunding campaigns have garnered worldwide attention, elevating their success to an unprecedented dimension, despite their previous achievements since 2014/15.

TERRAIN AND ENVIRONMENT

The assessment of terrain and environmental factors on battlefield performance is not as popular a topic as weapon systems, but it is always extremely important for any situation. However, the density of sensors (drones, optics, radars, etc.) on the battlefields in Ukraine has made some traditional benefits of terrain and environment obsolete.

It is not yet clear at the present time if this is a fundamental change, or if certain gaps in the skills of deployed combat troops also play a large role here. Armed forces around the world should avoid making hasty judgements or misinterpreting current trends.

The tactical assessment of wooded and broken terrain remains unchanged: there is enough concealment provided for dismounted forces especially to remain hidden even from the most modern systems. The same applies to combat in urban environments, with the added fact that here, as in previous centuries, we can expect drastically increased losses.

With regards to larger bodies of water, like the Dnieper, the principle has also not changed: it still takes a lot of effort to overcome these obstacles. If you try to cross with large equipment, you will quickly become a target for the enemy artillery. The destruction of the Kakhovka Dam on June 6, 2023 shows how eager both sides are to exploit such terrain factors to their advantage.

What is surprising, however, is the effectiveness with which the Ukrainian armed forces—without a proper Navy—now control movement in the western part of the Black Sea (see the weapons technology chapter).

The Russian force approach at the start of the invasion reveals that environmental factors did not appear to play a special role in the planning—as the battalion battle groups in the wooded north and in the Donetsk Basin in the east did not differ from each other. The Ukrainian Army, however, adapted their force disposition to the terrain—placing most of their infantry in the north, and most their mechanized forces in the east. So far, the weather has also given the fighting a certain rhythm: movements in the summer, some offensives in the fall before the muddy season (Russian: rasputiza), stationary fronts during the winter, preparations for offensives in the spring.

After the defensive successes of 2022, and the material aid from NATO, the question arose as to what geographical target a potential counter-offensive by Ukraine could have. The front line did not offer too many options, which is why the element of surprise hardly seemed possible. A mechanized offensive in 2023, aimed at advancing toward Crimea and splitting the Russian front, also met with limited success because of the enormous minefields created by the Russians. So what's next? Should the enemy feel safe while an amphibious landing is actually being planned to attack their flank or rear? Or are completely different options, or no options at all, being discussed by the Ukrainian General Staff? On the other hand, is a Russian breakthrough imminent? Only time will tell...

In addition to geographical conditions, we must now also understand the information space as an environmental factor. This war is being waged with targeted information and disinformation on both sides. For the first time, a major interstate war is taking place in which social media is massively involved and can even influence decisions within battles. Hundreds of thousands of civilians recorded Russian attack movements on cell phone videos and Ukrainian units could follow them live. The Ukrainian leadership has successfully weaponized the media as part of their defensive strategy to mobilize global opinion, while the Russian media initially made clumsy and somewhat outdated impressions.

"The mud at the bottom of the ditch was so sticky and deep that we had trouble walking. We had to quickly wipe our weapons clean or there would be interference from this thick mud. As soon as we broke into the trench, they tried to locate us with drones and dropped grenades on us. If they try that, we'll just shoot them with our rifles. They then fly low and slowly, making them easy to hit. When they fly past us, we leave them alone. Caring for the wounded was particularly difficult because we had to carry each wounded man over 200 meters through the mud in the trenches. But you have to run crouched because the ditches are not very deep and otherwise you are a target above the edge of the ditch. That was very tiring and took a long time."

Anonymous infantryman about trench warfare in a field in front of Bakhmut.

Trench warfare has experienced a powerful revival in Ukraine. Sometimes the images are reminiscent of trench warfare from the First World War, but with more modern weapons.

"Weather can be
a crucial obstacle
on the attack."

General Oleksandr Tarnavskyj,
Ukrainian commander.

TACTICAL FACTORS
INFANTRY

The troop genre that was decisive for the initial Ukrainian defense success was the infantry. At the beginning of the invasion, Ukraine's armed forces had a broad territorial infantry with light, unarmored vehicles. These forces are inexpensive and new units and task forces could quickly form after calling up reservists, as they require relatively little more than simple infantry weapons and motorization (usually pickups). These units could handle limited actions or conduct delaying operations by integrating various drone types and powerful tank defense rockets, especially in the forest and densely populated north of Ukraine. However, with their limited resources, they needed to either dig in or quickly get reinforced by heavier forces.

Since 2015, the Ukrainian armed forces have also introduced a medium-sized brigade type, which they have baptized in the best European tradition of "Jaeger Brigade". Since the beginning of the war, the 61st Brigade followed numerous other units which are mainly trained in forest and swamp fighting. Their equipment includes lightly armored vehicles, indirect fire and air support elements. In the first weeks of the war, units of these two categories, in cooperation with the special forces and mixed units of the National Guard, added significant losses to the Russian attack peaks in the Kiev area. The opponent had to terminate the attack on this front and regroup his forces.

This success not only surprised the public, but also military experts. Within military circles, a consensus seems to have prevailed before 2022 that infantry forces would not survive on the modern battlefield. Experts and the public were surprised not only by the success, but also by the repeated misjudgment that occurs every few decades. Success for such units depends on three key factors:

1. CAPABLE, DECENTRALIZED LEADERSHIP
2. DETERMINED, WELL-TRAINED TROOPS
3. USE OF MODERN TECHNOLOGIES AND TACTICS

The poorly prepared battle groups of the Russian battalion lacked sufficient infantry and proper training to effectively counter the Ukrainian troops. In the north there was therefore a series of ambush battles, which led to a temporary collapse of Russian front logistics.

The procedure was always comparable: a Ukrainian light infantry unit moves into position in favorable terrain, such as a town or a large forest area. It ensures that anti-tank defenses are placed in positions that can extensively overlook open terrain or streets. When all fire positions are clear, the soldiers get under the nearest safe cover—such as a basement. A drone and/or observation team is placed in a well camouflaged position to provide early detection of the opposing armored vehicles. When the opponent rolls into the prepared death zone, the ambush is triggered. Ideally, the first and last vehicles are knocked out first to make the rest of the column unable to maneuver. Once in the trap, the vehicle crews have little time to react or fight back effectively.

The mechanized heavy infantry in the country's west also fought hard, but did not have this combination of factors on its side. The more open terrain offered fewer opportunities here and the opponent's attacks were less predictable. The Ukrainian line of defense therefore had to be organized around the few natural obstacles—above all—the large bodies of water such as the Dnepr River. As in the Second World War, the Dnepr became the front line.

Since Ukraine has never had the means to wage war on a broad front, the infantry units began to dig in. If possible, they pulled mechanized infantry and tank troops from the front to ward off the opponent's attempts at breakthrough and to use them as a mobile reserve for their own counterattacks. Everyday war for the Ukrainian—and Russian—infantry can therefore quickly become trench warfare, which continues to this day. So far, the tactical situation has resulted in a strategic stalemate along the entire front, with the increased mobilization of the Russian state and western support for Ukraine keeping each other in check.

At the front, extensive field fortifications, artillery barrages and limited attacks by smaller units with short-range intermediate objectives exemplify the current situation. Both sides probe to find gaps in the opponent's defense without revealing weak points themselves. It is again the infantry that is important because they are easier to conceal than armored vehicles. The more the battle loses speed or even comes to a halt, the more important optical information systems (above all drones) and indirect fire weapon systems (artillery, mortar, etc.) become.

Nevertheless, any direct comparison with the trench warfare on the western front in World War I is inaccurate. Of course, Ukrainians and Russians fight over trenches and combat outposts. But such field fortifications have been a feature of almost every war since the American Civil War. Some of the excitement about this form of struggle shows how far western thinking has moved away from the realities of major intergovernmental combat. Furthermore, it is also very questionable about what purpose such comparisons should serve. Ultimately, only the pressure on journalists to generate click-throughs with the most dramatic headlines explains some of the overblown fascination with trench fighting.

The creation of field fortifications is a proven remedy for inferior forces to defend themselves against heavy enemy attacks (the old rule of thumb is that the attacker needs a 3:1 advantage in numbers hold true here). The deeper you dig in, the safer you are also against enemy artillery barrages, even with large calibers. Depending on the soil conditions and availability of building material for constructing trench walls and overhead cover, an infantry platoon can defend itself well against most attacks for three to six days. Such fortifications also permit a few soldiers at a time to man the fighting positions, while the rest of the unit is resting, cleaning weapons, collecting supplies, cooking food, or conducting other necessary activities.

Once an attack alarm is sounded, however, everyone can quickly move into the trenches to take up their defensive positions—and the enemy will face an attack against a largely unknown structure. With enough time and material, the defenders can construct extensive and deep lines of defense. This does not imply the need for trenches to be dug deeper and deeper into the ground, but rather the connection of dozens of such complexes in mutually supporting rows and layers. The enemy then must attack new trenches again and again at very short intervals while the defenders inflict loss upon loss on them until the attack is ground to a standstill. The speed of attack, which is inevitably slow, also gives the defender time to introduce reserves and create further defensive lines.

The depth of the Russian lines of defense in autumn 2023 in the front's south was about 30 kilometers. The defense features followed the Soviet pattern and included reinforced positions, concertina wire, trenches and extensive minefields (with up to five mines per square meter). Once an alley is cleared, the Russian artillery promptly carries out a new distance measurement from a distance. Since the mechanized brigades of Ukraine have suffered significant losses even with modern western equipment without making significant territorial gains, it is now the dismounted infantry that bears the main brunt of the fighting. On a wide front, shock troops attack in company-level strength to find weaknesses in the line to be exploited. Progress is slow but steady. Once a breakthrough occurs, the mechanized forces can rapidly push forward into enemy territory. The Russian defense shows signs however, that they lack enough forces in reserve for an effective counterattack, so they had to use forces such as the 76th Guards Air Assault Division, which were previously held in reserve, to actually just re-strengthen the front line.

Overall, there is an impression that many so-called teachings of the war are not all that new since February 2022. The successful ignorance of the war's nature caused western societies to have no idea of its reality at all. War is ugly, brutal, exhausting, and even minor victories have still the price of destroying families. Suitable weapons systems must be robust, simple, cost-effective and available in large enough numbers to make a difference. It is important to place all spare resources in hardened locations to protect them from shelling and drones. It is important that we conduct training as soon as possible and make it as long as necessary—with the greatest possible relevance for front use. Decentralized supply and repair structures must ensure that wounded soldiers and damaged equipment come back to the front as soon as possible. Wars require tremendous effort, solid leadership, and the will of the people to tough it out until victory. As in many wars before, in Ukraine, the fighting spirit of the infantry also seems to play a crucial role.

"It is necessary to place equipment on the floor and walls of the trench in order to work in this area. We have worked holes in the walls at short intervals and store some grenades and rifle ammunition there. So everyone can reload anytime and anywhere. We work in the main trench, then there is still a reserve trench and a protected trench. When the enemy tries to break in, we drive it into the trap with fire. He then sees that fire comes from two out of three trenches and decides for the third trench. Then our gifts are waiting for him. Our machine guns are never in a fixed position. We always bring them into use and give them the rest."

"Volod", infantry platoon leader in Donbass

"The Russians have a doctrine. Their tactic is the Soviet
doctrine. They still have the same guiding principle that
worked earlier. They just continue to apply it. Each unit
has an area that it has to take. First they come with
pioneers, sometimes for two or three days. They crawl in
front of our positions and search for mines. If they think
they have found a free way through, they prepare for the
attack. But they are too slow. We notice this and place our
mines right there. When they attack, the first step on the
mines. The rest then no longer want to attack. Sometimes
they take drugs, then a couple make it into the first
position. But then we smoke them out quickly. If we have
losses, it is from their artillery. This is much worse for us
than an infantry battle with rifles, machine guns and hand
grenades. For this you need some courage and the right
mindset to fight on despite fear. But if they come from
Wagner or are Chechen, it looks different. They know what
they are doing. Fighting against them is very hard."

"Varr", 28-year-old, leader of an infantry company in Donbass
on January 3, 2023

"When I got to the front for the first time, I almost shit my pants. If you are not afraid here, you are either an idiot or dead the next day."

"Santa", militia leader

"There is too little forest in the south, which makes it difficult for us to fight. As a result, we cannot move so much and have hardly any building materials for the field fortifications. We must take everything from ruined buildings or from the residents. It was better in the Donbass."

"Viking", leader of a light infantry company

"After the mobilization started, I fled to Mongolia. Then I was able to get to Ukraine via Turkey and report to the Siberian battalion. Someone has to stop these criminals."

"Vargan", member of the Siberian battalion of the Ukrainian army, Russian citizen from Yakutia.

The media portrayed the German Leopard tanks as a potential miracle weapon for Ukraine. However, this could not be the case because of the small number that were delivered–the Leopard tanks did significantly increase the survival prospects for Ukrainian tank crews though.

TANKS

6

Both warring parties use armored battle vehicles. The war in Ukraine is the first real tank war on European soil since World War II. Already in the first year of the war, so-called experts overturned with polarizing assessments about the end or the future of the tank as a weapon system on the battlefield. Only one thing is certain: the (fighting) tank will neither disappear nor mutate into the all-decisive weapon of war. In order to understand why the tank is so important for the battle in Ukraine and how there can be such great losses, we need to take a closer look at the weapon systems used and the conditions within which they are being used.

In Ukraine, both sides use variants of the T-series which are Soviet designs that have sometimes undergone modifications or been manufactured after 1990, and were specifically designed for use by armies of conscripts. The Soviet combat doctrine was based around the mass use of tanks in war to defeat the technical superiority of Western weapon systems through sheer numerical superiority. The Soviet leadership saw this as a logical strategy, considering their success in defeating the German Wehrmacht during 'The Great Patriotic

War' (WWII) with this approach. For such a doctrine to be effective, the armored vehicles had to be relatively simple and cheap to mass produce, and able to replace damaged, or destroyed vehicles quickly. They also had to be easy to use to keep the training time short for the crews. In addition, the tanks also needed speed and maneuverability on the battlefield and had to be comparatively light. Finally, they had to have great firepower to defeat Western tanks. Since a combat tank is always a compromise of firepower, mobility and tank protection, advantages in one factor always come along with disadvantages in another one.

The T-series fully met these goals, but they do not use them in this sense in Ukraine. Unlike the Soviet doctrine, the Russians did not use tanks for the first few days of their massed attack, or by the next wave. Instead, they chose to deploy into battle in small units or individually to duel against Ukrainian tanks or infantry. The use of isolated single tanks or small groups without infantry support can be tactically very unfavorable and devastating for any tank.

In addition, there are aspects of maintenance and repair. The overall lifespan of the tank and the maintenance of individual components received little to no attention because no one ever planned for a T-72 tank to fire several hundred shots over many months and drive thousands of kilometers. So, the tanks were designed with cheap mass production in mind, neglecting durability or ease of maintenance or repair. For example, to change the engine of a T-series tank is a task that takes several days—while a Leopard 2 can be rolling back into battle with a new drive unit within an hour. Western tanks crews are also much more thoroughly trained than their Soviet / Russian counterparts—making them more effective in combat.

Regarding the various tank models from T-64 to T-90, it should be noted that the numerical sequence creates the impression of larger differences between them than what actually exists. These are less generational jumps (as from Leopard 1 to 2) than evolutionary steps within a generation. Both the Russian and the Ukrainian armies mainly use T-72 variants. With its 125-millimeter cannon and upgraded fire control system (especially in the Russian B3 variant), this battle tank has a considerable firepower. The approximately 42-ton vehicle (weight dependent upon variant) is powered by the multi-fuel engine with 840 hp, which allows it to run on different types of fuel. By comparison, the Leopard 2 has almost twice the engine output, but weighs at least 20 tons more, which is a disadvantage to mobility under certain ground conditions.

Three crew members are required for the operation of the T-72: commander, gunner, and driver. An automatic loading system replaced the loader crew member that is used in most Western tanks. On the one hand, reducing the total weight and silhouette of the vehicle was possible—especially in height. On the other hand, one less person is available for tasks such as maintenance and shift operation. Additionally, the charging carousel in the turret ring houses half of the ammunition supply, which consists of 22 cartridges. So if there is a penetration of the turret (for example from above, where the armor is weak), the probability is very high that the ammunition will detonate. In this case, the entire crew and the tank will be lost. Moreover, the turret often gets blown into the air–a spectacle that gained considerable media attention in the Iraq War in 1991, and again in Ukraine in 2022.

Improper use can also explain the high losses of combat armor, especially on the Russian side. They are not utilizing their tanks as intended, which is to work alongside other weapons, especially in complex terrains with infantry support, and in significant quantities. Unless tanks move rapidly, catch the enemy off guard, and triumph on the battlefield, they can be easily engaged by a range of weapons systems. This was first felt by the two groups of forces in the attack on the capital Kiev–which, together with the air landing at Hostomel, should have brought about an early victory for the Russians. However, unlike in 2014, the Ukrainian forces did not try to stop the strong, armored opponent directly at the border, but allowed it to advance and then attacked the follow-on forces behind the main advance. At the same time, intelligence about movement profiles and strength compositions was being collected. The sight of completely destroyed columns of Russian vehicles was primarily possible because the actual defense only started when the BTGs could not be re-supplied and ground to a halt after a few days. The use of time and depth to exploit and create weakness and confusion among the Russian attackers was effectively carried out by mobile infantry units with modern anti-armor weapons.

Another interesting feature of the fighting in Ukraine is that the latest infantry fighting vehicle and tank models of the Russian armed forces do not yet seem to have been able to be used at the front. We have hardly seen any deployments of the T-14 Armata and BMPT Terminator at the front. Moreover, in August 2023, the Russian armed forces reportedly completely withdrew the T-14 from the front.

Lastly, the Russians probably also need all components for the replenishment and replacement of armored vehicle depots. To what extent China can provide all the critical components for the latest Russian systems is unclear. Previously, many components for optics and electronics sector came from France, but these are now blocked because of sanctions and embargoes.

It is reasonable to assume that the Ukrainians will continue to rely on a wide selection of combat vehicles for several years. If the Russian aggression continues, Ukraine will certainly produce Western weapon systems locally. Within NATO, the delivery of older battle tanks and fighting vehicles, as well as a general rethink, has led to considerable new procurements. Poland is at the forefront in this regard. The country has already signed contracts to manufacture 1,000 Korean combat tanks in a Polish version locally. There are large quantities of fighting vehicles and armored personnel carriers in their plans as well.

The Ukrainian summer offensive of 2023 began with high hopes as they employed Western tanks, including the Leopard 2, for the first time. The Western tanks, of course, could not meet the completely exaggerated expectations of Western politicians. Analysis of the vehicles' performance and the tactics used will probably continue for many years. But in view of the extent of the conflict, the tactical framework of the front and the small number of pieces delivered, no serious expert could expect them to have had a crucial influence on the offensive.

Such deliveries to Ukraine certainly give the country the ability to keep up the fight against the Russian onslaught, and sometimes this is all that is needed for a later victory. At this point, we can say that the battle tank is vulnerable, but it is still the best offensive weapon for capturing ground. The tank arrived on the battlefields of the Western Front over a century ago, but it still looks set to stay—it will only continue to change and adapt.

Today, soldiers can recognize an armored tip of attack in three to five minutes and fight it in another three minutes. Successful movements on the battlefield can only be achieved if they are completed in less than 10 minutes. Under these conditions, it is extremely difficult to achieve surprise against the opponent."

Major General Wadym Skibitskyj, commander of the Military Intelligence Service of Ukraine

"There will most likely not be a deep and successful breakthrough."

General Valerii Zaluzhnyi, Commander-In-Chief of the Ukrainian Armed Forces, in November 2023.

"The artillery is the king of the battlefield, the infantry the queen. When the two conceived a child, the mortar was born."

"Matros" has been serving for several years on a mortar team in eastern Ukraine.

ARTILLERY

7

The Russian army can fall back on a gigantic amount of gun and ammunition stocks from Soviet times. The predominant mass of artillery weapons used is therefore, of older design. Although towed guns were still or are still in existence, self-propelled guns have been available in large quantities in the Soviet and Russian army for decades. Use of the 2S3 is particularly widespread, with at least 10,000 examples having been manufactured since the 1970s. But also more modern systems such as the 2S19, manufactured at the end of the 1980s, were available in their hundreds at the beginning of the war. In addition, there are various mechanized, large-caliber mortar systems—up to 240 millimeter—and heavy guns. Lastly, the Russian armed forces have an enormous pool of light vehicles for fire support, particularly the 2S1.

The Ukrainian army also uses most of these types. The war is primarily being fought with obsolete Soviet artillery across various fronts. Despite this, both parties strive to employ their most effective systems in their respective domains. On the Ukrainian side, these are primarily western guns, especially the German Panzer-haubitze 2000.

Although this weapon system is also a child of the 1980s and emerged from the failed development history of the PZH 70, it is unique in at least one aspect to this day: the PZH 2000 is MRSI-compatible (Multi-Round-Si-multaneous-Impact). This means it can fire several shells in succession, which all then strike at the same time. As the self-propelled howitzer does not have a ground spade, it absorbs the recoil forces evenly into the ground through the tracks, which allows it to change position at the time of impact. This speed, which no other systems have achieved yet, ensures a high level of survivability by drastically reducing the risk of counterfire from the enemy. In this way, the few 2000s delivered can still af-fect the Ukrainian side with a persistently positive effect.

However, even with all the technological superiority of the Western weapons systems, the long-lasting intensity of the fighting has also revealed several weaknesses. Despite the best tactical employment, there have been losses and the high unit cost, combined with low produc-tion capacities, of these systems means that cannot cover all the needs at the front. Even the largest manufactur-ers in the United States face considerable challenges in producing enough of these weapons quickly enough to meet the tactical requirements of the Ukrainians. On the other hand, the armaments industry of the Russian Feder-ation also faces many constraints but has found a strong and reliable partner in China—who can offer everything from raw materials to weapons development and final production. In the current war of attrition, whichever side can produce and replenish more weapons systems (and trained combat personnel) than the other will achieve dominance.

Another complication factor is that both sides use a wide mix of weapon types and calibers. The Ukrainian Armed Forces particularly have to cope with a wide variety of systems and calibers, as it uses both former Warsaw Pact and NATO weapons. Under these circumstances, a particularly well-functioning logistics system for stockpiling, maintaining, and supplying arms, ammunition and spare parts obviously needs to be in place. Even within NATO standard calibers, there can be individual differences between such things as the charges for artillery shells that can cause damage to a weapon if used incorrectly. The Ukrainian Armed Forces have therefore set up their own facility to test compatibility and safety, and to ensure harmonization between various weapons and ammunition types—and in order to provide simple and clear instructions for their troops. These unbureaucratic, decentralized communication channels are quite efficient in many places.

The most cost-effective indirect fire weapon on the battlefield is the mortar. It is an omnipresent weapon on the Ukrainian-Russian front lines. Mortars are usually integrated into infantry companies or battalions for organic fire support. Personnel can quickly learn how to use mortars effectively, as their operation is simple and straightforward. The range is much shorter than howitzers, which are usually part of the artillery forces, however. Even a large-caliber mortar with a 120mm pro-jectile has a maximum range of only about six kilometers. To effectively fire on enemy positions, mortar squads position themselves directly behind, or even within, the front lines. Mortar crews are therefore also trained as regular infantry riflemen as well. If necessary, they must be able to engage in close-range direct combat in the event of an enemy breakthrough. Over the past 30 years, many NATO forces have increasingly cut or dismantled funding and training for indirect fire support in frontline companies, or simply neglected to provide them with new modern weapons. The delivery of larger quantities of older NATO weapons to Ukraine has now sped up the development of new procurement programs in several countries.

On the Russian side, their forces also have comparable, albeit less precise, indirect fire systems, such as their counterpart to the HIMARS known as the BM-30 Smerch. In addition, Russian Navy and the Air Force aircraft have enough range—especially with aerial refueling—to launch from bases beyond the range of Ukrainian artillery and at-tack objectives anywhere across the entire Ukrainian ter-ritory. Faced with this precarious situation, the Ukrainian logistics set up proved to quite resilient because of its decentralized and dispersed emplacement. As a result, Russian forces switched to attacking civilian facilities and infrastructure instead of military targets. Especially for countries that do not have, or cannot afford, a powerful air force, investing in long-range rocket artillery can be a suitable alternative, at least in situations where the rockets would have sufficient range to reach significant targets in enemy territory.

Despite using outdated weapons, the Ukrainians have implemented an effective network of guns, real-time drone reconnaissance, and target identification and assignment through a Battle Management System. By significantly enhancing their reaction speed, they can effectively defend the front line against any attack. The system quickly detects any attack, and the enemy forces cannot advance quickly enough to avoid artillery fire. The Russians have been observing and adopting the practices of the Ukrainians, and they have started implementing similar systems and processes themselves. This is an essential reason why the front lines have been in pretty much in a stalemate situation as of the autumn of 2023.

To draw any sweeping general conclusions about wars in the near or distant future from the current situation in Ukraine would be fundamentally wrong. The course of conflicts is determined by so many different factors that accurate predictions are not possible. Sun Tzu's description of the general principles of war is the only applicable approach. The future of artillery warfare is therefore uncertain, however, the Ukraine situation confirms much established knowledge.

"The PZH 2000 is superior to other systems in many aspects. Modern armor and the ammunition storage separated from the crew gives us security and trust in the gun concept. We can live and work for days within the gun and constantly change position. Due to the loading machine and the fire control system, we are ten times faster than with our old Pion 2S7. As a rule, we release three shots in ten seconds and have already changed the position when the Russians discover us. Here in Bakhmut I take around 60 to 100 grenades a day, mainly in opposing fire on enemy artillery."

"Oleksii", gun commander of a tank shaft 2000 of the 43rd artillery groom on March 13, 2023 near Bakhmut.

"The Russian artillery fires without a break. You can't stay in one place, you have to move. Movement is life."

Andrej, infantryman somewhere in the Zaporishija region in the summer of 2023.

The Wagner Group is a Russian private military company (security contractors, or mercenaries–depending on one's perspective) that acted as a replacement force for the Russian Army. Here we see an example of a propaganda leaflet for the so-called "musicians".

SPECIAL OPERATIONS FORCES

The Ukrainian special forces have now almost completely transformed away from their Spetsnaz background during the Soviet era. Various Ukraine units have also been trained by elite NATO special units over the past decade as well; such as, the British Special Air Service, US Army Special Forces and others. In the process, Ukrainian special units have achieved a complete realignment according to NATO standards. In addition, much of the equipment they now use is standard issue to most international SOF units, for example, the GPNVG (Ground Panoramic Night Vision Goggle) from L3 Harris. On January 5, 2016, the Ukrainian Army established the Ukrainian Army Special Forces (UASOF) as a separate unit, emphasizing their strategic independence and classic SF task profile.

The operational core comprises the 3rd and 8th Separate Special Purpose Regiments, each of which has three to four companies. Added to this are the commando frogmen groups, consisting of three specialized platoons. The 61st Jäger Brigade, which was set up in 2019, also supports the SF units as a specialized light infantry brigade, similar to the 75th Ranger Regiment of the United States Army. In 2020, NATO certified the 3rd Separate Special Purpose Regiment, and a year later, US Navy Seals trained the Ukrainian commando frogmen. Around the same time, they introduced a new tough selection process based on Western standards. Only about 20 percent of volunteers successfully complete the six-month-long selection process and are accepted for advanced training. The greatest support for Ukrainian special forces has come from British and U.S. forces over the past decade. According to leaked Pentagon documents, the British have the strongest contingent (at least 50 men) of special forces trainers in Ukraine. By normal standards, this is quite a high number for special units to have in-country.

At least since the spring of 2022, Western Special Forces have had a special reason for taking a keen interest in their Ukrainian comrades. Ukrainian SOF units are currently the only Western special forces that have actual campaign experience in a large, intergovernmental war. The ability for Western SOF units to gain first-hand knowledge is therefore extremely valuable. Of course, the missions of these units are naturally top secret, and even if Western forces were also participating in combat as well as conducting training, there would be no way to confirm it officially.

However, some clues are available. It is certain that special forces teams decisively supported the defense of the Kiev area by Ukrainian territorial and regular Army units and the regular army—and also most notably in defense against the Russian air landing at Hostomel. In an interview in November 2022, the then commander of UASOF, Viktor Khorenko, described the operational concept of the command. Each unit has been allocated to specific border regions, and the special forces soldiers consistently train alongside the territorial infantry, enabling them to become intimately familiar with the area and choose optimal positions for defense and offense in advance. Because of their thorough preparation, they were able to respond effectively to the Russian attack, ultimately influencing the outcome in a significant way. There is ample visual evidence showcasing the effective collaboration between Ukrainian special forces and frontline units in achieving tactical success, following their initial defensive triumphs. If this information is accurate, it would minimize the waste and maximize the strategic impact of Ukrainian special forces. Special forces should always possess the potential to have a significant strategic effect—otherwise, they would be ineffective due to their limited numbers.

The well-equipped SF troops say they fight almost exclusively at night because this gives them a significant advantage over the regular Russian troops, who do not have individual night vision devices. Furthermore, Ukrainian commando units might have been responsible for some of the destruction of important infrastructure and depots in Crimea and southwest Russia. In contrast to other wars, there is no language barrier here, so clandestine infiltration by special units is much easier on both sides. There are also said to have been numerous

missions by UASOF against infiltrating Russian sabo-
teurs, to support the special units of the Ukrainian police
("Omega", "Alpha" and "Vega").

The Ukrainian SOF units have made an especially noticeable impact in the Black Sea area. Ukrainian
commando frogmen have recaptured some oil rigs off
Crimea and are successfully deploying new maritime
drones that pose a tremendous threat to the Russian
Black Sea Fleet. Frigates and destroyers worldwide are
currently still inadequately defended against small and
fast surface drones. These are probably also in covert
operational use in Crimea, providing target data for missile and air strikes. In the autumn of 2023, Ukrainian
maritime drones destroyed a Russian submarine in dry
dock and to hit the Russian Black Sea Fleet headquarters
during an operational briefing meeting.

In addition to the professional special forces, there
are a whole range of other special units in the Ukrainian
Armed Forces, which do not correspond to the Western
definition of elite forces. For example, it is possible to
assume that small teams or individual SF trainers aim to
establish partisan movements across the Russian Federation in order to engage and distract Russian forces. The
numerous attacks on Russian infrastructure as far away
as Siberia could have been conducted in this way. Depending on how the further course of the war is shaped
and how it ends, we may uncover details about Ukrainian
commando operations in a few years' time.

In November 2023, Commander Viktor Khorenko, who
had been highly successful, was removed from his po-

sition as UASOF commander with the explanation that he was required for a special assignment. There is no doubt that the precise significance of this will remain unclear for some time.

"We make use of the latest maps, including ones that are just a few months old, and have the capability to digitally edit any information as needed. At Russian command posts, we stumbled upon maps sourced from old Soviet Spetsnaz manuals. It is common however for Russian commanders to misuse their elite Spetsnaz forces by simply sending them to fight as light infantry in the trenches. We on the other hand mainly carry out all classic battle missions of special operations forces— around the clock. From hand-to-hand action against strategically relevant weapon systems, to long-distance recon inserts, to the formation of partisan units. My men haven't had a break since the beginning of the war. It is very hard."

Viktor Khorenko, commander of UASOF from July 2022 to November 2023

THE INTERNATIONAL LEGION

Foreign factions have also been engaged in combat on behalf of Ukraine since 2014. These were primarily anti-Russian or other politically motivated fighters from Eastern Europe and the Caucasus. The first organization with perceptible recruitment success was the Georgian Legion, which still exists and comprises about half Georgians and half foreigners from other nations. In November 2023, observers estimated the size of the group to be that of a reinforced battalion, comprising between 800 and 1,000 men. Many Chechens have also formed several groups since 2014 and continue to have an influx of recruits to form several small battalions.

With the Russian invasion in 2022, the Ukrainian leadership also utilized the attention of the world's public media to recruit members, primarily from western countries, when they founded the international legion. To date, it is unclear how many fighters have actually registered for service in Ukraine. According to research by the "New York Times" in early 2023, the International Legion seemed to comprise a maximum of 3,000 fighters. However, Ukrainian leadership spoke of 20,000–although it was not clear if this was only the number of applicants rather than actual signed-up fighters. Up to now, relatives from Canada, the USA and Great Britain have featured particularly prominently, but there are also members from all western countries in the combat area. Behind the legionnaires are often crowdfunding initiatives (such as the Canadian "Black Maple Company"), which ensure the financing of a living in the home country and the purchase of equipment. Many share their experiences on social media and generate direct support there. It is also noticeable that some fighters from western countries have returned home after a short time and complained about unprofessional conduct of Ukrainian officers. It is impossible to check whether these statements are true or if military laypersons wanted to conceal their own poor conduct by making such statements.

With the progression of the war, Russian militias that fight against the Russian army have also appeared. They include organizations such as the ultra-nationalist Russian volunteer corps, which includes well-known neo-Nazis. Together with the Legion "Free Russia", this organization became known for its raids on the Russian region of Belgorod from May 2023.

From an organizational point of view, the quantity of the various groups is very confusing and, of course, is also subject to quite high personnel fluctuation. Such units are often associated with their own cult of followers and thus have an attractive effect on certain layers of society. Even if most of these associations lead to the name "battalion" in the name, they are often only smaller groups in platoon or company strength- about 30 or 100 men. To avoid large combat losses from these contingents, the Ukrainians likely deploy international units in the second or third line of combat, so as not to endanger Western support.

While not a direct component of the International Legion, there is a company of the Ukrainian special forces which is comprised of foreigners—probably recruited from the best fighters of the international contingents.

WAGNER GROUP (PMC)

From 2014, the Russian side also created new armed units. The first well-known use of the mercenary "Wagner Group" took place in Donbas. Usually, they recruited personnel from the ranks of former soldiers of the Russian army, mostly in the age band between 30 and 50 years, and within a few years, the force had grown to a strength of several thousand. The organization established itself as a politically credible military power extension of the Russian Federation in Syria and large parts of Central Africa, while also setting up smaller training and consulting squads in Venezuela and Sri Lanka.

In order to deny a connection with official Russian armed forces, the group largely operated in the shadows and did not allow the possession of devices with internet connection, for example. In addition, confidentiality declarations had to be signed for ten years. The promise of better pay and a slightly elite reputation attracted plenty of Russian ex-soldiers over the years, mostly with war experience from Chechnya. After the initial invasion of Ukraine failed, the number of Wagner fighters on the front grew continuously until it reached at least ten thousand men. Ukrainian soldiers saw the mercenaries as tough opponents, and they came up against them in numerous battles. Wagner troops even took on the central role in the fight for Bakhmut. By that time however, most Wagner fighters were now former prison inmates, and the Group also suffered enormous losses at the front. Individual reports show that the long-serving, experienced Wagner fighter used these new recruits to draw Ukrainian fire before launching their actual attack.

The Wagner organization is connected to numerous war crimes in both Ukraine and Africa. Conditions within the group are also extremely harsh even by Russian standards: in September 2022, a leaked video showed the brutal execution, by sledgehammer, of a Wagner mercenary who had allegedly deserted. It was also only at this point that Yevgeny Prigozhin acknowledged himself as the leader of the organization, while it is likely that former GRU officer Dmitri Utkin led the Group's military operations. Utkin's long-standing combat call-sign "Wagner" is also what gave the group its name. Although Prigozhin received significantly more media attention, Utkin, with his openly National Socialist tendencies, was regarded as the most crucial figure in shaping the identity and service record of the group.

Although the Wagner group never achieved such importance that it could have seriously challenged the power of the Russian army, the staging of a coup attempt in 2023 was enough of a threat to bring about the downfall and restructuring of the organization. Both Prigozhin and Utkin were killed for their role in the coup attempt when their private jet was shot down by the Russians on August 23, 2023. The shooting down of their plane was presumably on Putin's orders.

"After our comrades broke through the first line, we were ordered to attack a neighboring Russian platoon. We jumped into the enemy trenches and encountered a dozen men, armed only with shovels. They felt confused about their whereabouts and the ongoing events. One of them quickly spoke up and told us they were all in a prison in Russia yesterday. They had been recruited from prison and sent directly to the front lines at Bakhmut. They knew nothing about the war and had received no training or instructions—they had literally been sitting in prison since before the invasion of Ukraine. Their commanders simply put them into the trenches and told them they were meat for the grinder. All the regular Wagner troops had withdrawn from the lines and laid land mines between their positions and the trenches. These men had simply been abandoned. Some of us wanted to beat them up to avenge our comrades, but I just felt sorry for them. That's why I held our troops back."

S. Penduk, infantryman in the battle of Bakhmut.

"After taking the other bank, we thought the Russians would flee and we could bring supplies and reinforcements over—but it didn`t work out that way. Instead, they threw everything they had at us—artillery, mortars, and even flame-throwers. I thought I would never get out of that situation. Our replenishment was the weak point. The Russians monitored and bombarded our resupply routes and it became increasingly difficult. We had no food or drinking water for a while, even though we tried everything we could with boats and drones."

Anonymous Ukrainian marine infantryman at the crossing of the Dnieper River at Krynky.

"If you think you are prepared for everything, you are wrong. Our attack started and suddenly there was a huge, black cloud. Hundreds of thousands of bees were over us—my men just ran. I don't know if it was intentional, but the ‚Orcs‘ had shot up all the beehives. While we retreated, they also withdrew. It was surreal."

"Pole", platoon leader in the 128th Mountain Infantry Brigade.

"If it is really hard and we have a lot of losses, I tell the men that they have to do what I do myself: ask yourself what you are here for. Why do you have to be here now and endure this? Every artillery impact of the Russians makes me angry. I get angry every day. There are enough opportunities to get even, and we use them all."

Major Roman Kovalev, Battalion Commander in November 2022

THE WAR OF THE FUTURE 9

Just a few years ago, the discussion of military details was not at all socially acceptable in many Western societies. Today, the media inundates us with statements about what is supposedly happening at the front. In the coffee shop or at the bakery, people discuss whether HIMARS or Taurus is the better "miracle weapon" for Ukraine, for example.

Yet despite the thousands of images and videos available, the public still only has a very limited insight into the operational reality on the Ukrainian-Russian front. The surprise of the (western) media about the mass use of guided missiles, tanks, artillery, and the reduction of mobile combat to trench warfare must surely make professional personnel chuckle ironically. Professional personnel must find the media's surprise amusing because these facets of war are well established and have been used for decades.

Also, everyone believes we must learn from this conflict. But one should ask: What can, and should, NATO actually learn from the Ukraine war? Just because something works, or not, for the Ukrainian or Russian armed forces in this combat environment does not mean that it's a universal truth. Also, nobody can calculate who will lose, who will win, or how the war will end. Warfare is much less a science than an art—albeit a hideous one. Throughout history, no group or nation has been able to secure permanent victories in advance either. The future is an undiscovered country, as the old saying goes.

There are a few aspects that quite new to this war though. This includes the enormous integration of social media into the propaganda machine. The Ukrainian side in particular can celebrate immense success here, which has resulted directly in foreign weapons aid. A big factor, civil and military, was also the decentralized Starlink network, which is indispensable for Ukrainian information processing. The mass use of disposable drones also marks a new facet: currently the Ukrainian armed forces are probably using up to 10,000 drones per month on the front. The influence of the use of artificial intelligence on war is currently not foreseeable.

Just as combat in the 20th century was dominated by aircraft and tanks, war in the 21st century seems to be dominated by unmanned systems and artificial intelligence—and we are only just beginning to understand what this means for operational doctrine and combat training. However, amidst all these changes, we should not forget that classic virtues of victorious armies, such as determination, courage, and taking responsibility, will continue to exist in the future. Those who can connect established methods with innovative tools will also be well-prepared for future conflicts.

"The Ukrainian Armed Forces can only break through the current patient situation in the war of attrition against Russia through new skills and technologies. Russia will keep the numerical and material superiority in the foreseeable future. We need a quick victory, we cannot win a war of attrition."

Valerii Zaluzhnyi, Commander-In-Chief of the Ukrainian Armed Forces until being replaced in February 2024.

TEN LESSONS FROM THE UKRAINE WAR

1. ALWAYS REMAIN FLEXIBLE

Only those who can quickly ascertain and understand the situation will be successful on the modern battlefield. The digital battlefield demands maximum flexibility.

2. ALWAYS LEAD WITH DETERMINATION

In the rigors of battle, determined leadership at all levels must clearly convey why sacrifices are necessary and what goals can and should be achieved.

3. WEAPON TECHNOLOGY SHOULD BE MODULAR

The armaments of the future will have to adapt faster to changing conditions. This requires modular hardware that allows significant changes to the weapon system through software modifications in a few months.

4. STRENGTH NEEDS STRENGTH

Armed Forces must be available for national defense efforts and not just as an expedition corps in distant countries. A revived dimension is needed, involving a comprehensive reserve and mobilization organization, as well as functional division and corps structures.

5. MATERIEL NEEDS QUANTITY

If something is good enough, there is a need for more of it. From rifles to bridges, there will be damage and losses sustained. Inventory will have to be replenished, so the armaments industry must be able to sustain regular orders to maintain or increase production.

6. INFANTRY IS CRUCIAL

Even in the 21st century and in the face of new technologies, it is still the infantryman who takes and holds territory. Every nation needs a large amount of well-trained infantry units with modern equipment to guarantee success in battle.

7. NOTHING SUCCEEDS WITHOUT TANKS

If you want to break through fortified enemy lines, you need armored combat vehicles. They may have become more vulnerable, but there is still no real alternative for offensive ground combat operations.

8. RECONNAISSANCE IS EVERYTHING

Today's possibilities for situational awareness, thanks to everything from small hand-launched drones to satellites in space, enable enormous clarity of the battlefield picture. Anyone who falters here is wielding a dull sword or a weak shield. Anyone who neglects electronic warfare today is fighting a losing battle.

9. MORE PRECISION IN DEPTH

When we identify tactically or strategically significant goals, we need to be able to strike quickly and precisely. Powerful precision artillery is essential.

10. ALWAYS REMAIN OPEN-MINDED

Armed forces that encourage thinking in new directions and trying out new things will pave the way for the future. Whoever forgets the lessons of the past will also fall behind.

FURTHER READING

THE BATTALION TACTICAL GROUP

A rational analysis of the battle performance of the Russian battalion-tactical group (BTG). The authors from the Theresian Military Academy compare between the use of these formations in 2014 and 2023 and clarify the concept's failure in Ukraine.

"Russia's battalion-tactical groups in operational planning and tactical efforts in the war for Ukraine 2014 to 2023"
by Markus Reisner and Christian Hahn, de Gruyter, 2023, 14 pages, free essay available online:
http://tinyurl.com/2b9mf6d4

RUSSIAN REGULAR GROUND FORCES ORDER OF BATTLE

This essay comprises two parts: an introductory essay on the regular Russian ground troops and a complete battle order (ORBAT) of the regular Russian ground troops down to the brigade and regiment level (with selected independent battalions), including the Army, the ground troops controlled by the Navy, of the air landing units (VDV) and the GRU Spetsnaz formations.

"Russian Regular Ground Forces Order of Battle: Russian Military 101",

by Mason Clark and Carolina Hird, Understanding War, 2023, 60 pages, free essay available online: http://tinyurl.com/29p4u2bv

MEAT GRINDER: RUSSIAN TACTICS

The armed forces of the Russian Federation facing NATO systems in 2022, which they had not previously encountered, caused a significant deviation in Russian operations from the Russian doctrine, leading to the extent of Russian losses. This report should show how the Russian armed forces have adapted their tactics in the Ukraine conflict and what challenges have arisen for the Ukrainian military.

"Meat Grinder: Russian Tactics in the Second Year of its Invasion of Ukraine",

by Jack Watling and Nick Reynolds , RUSI, 2023, 27 pages, free essay available online:

http://tinyurl.com/2dm2rxfb

MODERN POSITIONAL WARFARE AND HOW TO WIN IT

It is rare that the Commander-In-Chief of an army at war publishes a technical essay on the current situation while the battle is still running. Zaluzhnyi strategic assessment describes the war in November 2023 as a stalemate situation, which could only be broken by enormous expansion of existing skills and the use of completely new technologies.

"Modern Positional Warfare and how to win it ",

by Valerii Zaluzhnyi, published in "The Economist" in November 2023, 9 pages, free essay available online: http://tinyurl.com/yo32n9s8

THE FIGHT FOR THE INITIATIVE

A few days prior to his dismissal, Valerii Zaluzhnyi, the Commander-In-Chief of the Ukrainian Armed Forces, described in an article the change in the war in Ukraine. In this article, he analyzed how the country needed to adapt in order to continue successfully defending itself. SPARTANAT documented Zaluzhnyi "the fight for the initiative" in German translation.

"The fight for the initiative. On the modern conception of military operations in the Russian-Ukrainian War"

*by Valerii Zaluzhnyi, published in German on SPARTANAT, freely available essay in the appendix in German translation or **online at: https://tinyurl.com/2cxok3f6***

ZOV – DER VERBOTENE BERICHT

Pavel Filatiev no longer lives in Russia, but in exile in France. This is no surprise considering his book. Anyone who wonders about the poor "performance" of the Russian troops will get a lot of anecdotal information from Filatiev. He took part in the storming of Kherson for the first two months of the war. In the first book from the Russian side there is a lot of "fog of war", there is chaos, and the paratroopers are, as Pavel Filatiev describes, just a shadow of the elite troops they once were.

"ZOV – Der verbotene Bericht. Ein russischer Fallschirmjäger packt aus"

by Pavel Filatiev, published in German by Hoffmann & Campe Verlag, Hamburg 2022, 190 pages. Also available for Kindle and as an audio book.

SCHÜTZENHILFE: FÜR DIE UKRAINE IM KRIEG

Here it comes, the experiential literature: Moved by the images of the war of aggression, the trained armored infantryman Jonas Kratzenberg decides to support the Ukrainian people in their struggle for freedom—as a soldier, in armed combat. He joins the International Legion.

"Schützenhilfe: Für die Ukraine im Krieg—ein deutscher Soldat berichtet von der Front"

by Jonas Kratzenberg, YES Verlag, Munich 2023, 224 pages. Also available for Kindle and as an audio book.

WAR IN UKRAINE

The Helion Company (UK) paperback series "Europe at War" has published several volumes on the war in Ukraine. The titles currently available on Amazon are:

"War in Ukraine (1): Armed Formations of the Donetsk People's Republic, 2014-2022" (Europe@war, 21, Volume 1)

"War in Ukraine (2): Russian Invasion, February 2022" (Europe@war, 28, Volume 2)

"War in Ukraine (3): Armed Formations of the Luhansk People's Republic 2014-2022" (Europe@war, 33, Volume 3)

"War in Ukraine (4): Main Battle Tanks of Russia and Ukraine, 2014-2023: Soviet Legacy and Post-Soviet Russian MBTs" (Europe@war, 35, Volume 4)

"War in Ukraine (5): Main Battle Tanks of Russia and Ukraine, 2014-2023; Post-Soviet Ukrainian MBTs and Combat Experience" (Europe@war, 36, Volume 5).

THE RUSSO-UKRAINIAN WAR

"The Russo-Ukrainian War" is the comprehensive story of a war that has raged since 2014 and, with Russia's attempt to take Kiev, shattered a geopolitical order that had been cemented since the end of the Cold War.

"The Russo-Ukrainian War"
by Serhii Plokhy, Penguin Publishing, London 2023, 385 pages. Also available for Kindle and as an audio book.

LEARN MORE

The American website "Understanding War" brings up-to-date reports on conflicts worldwide and also accompanies the war in Ukraine with extensive reports daily: *www.understandingwar.org*

On the Russian side, the "Rybar" channel reports on the Ukrainian war—from a Russian perspective, of course: *www.rybar.ru*

If you not only want to read but also apply it, you can take an apprenticeship directly with the author of this book. The "Lehrmanufaktur" by and with Christian Väth offers the "Strategy & Tactics" seminar.
Lehrmanufaktur: *www.lehrmanufaktur.com/lehre*

Practical course formats on this topic are available under the Light Infantry International brand: Combat Mindset, Leadership, Tactics, Shooting Training, Fitness and more.
Light Infantry International: *www.lightinfantry.de*

For all "students of war" and those who prefer to just listen, there is the "Strategy & Tactics Podcast" on Patreon. Free trial subscriptions are available, contains lots of in-depth content.
Strategy & Tactics Podcast: *www.patreon.com/LightInfantryInternational*

ABOUT THE AUTHOR:

CHRISTIAN VÄTH

founded "Light Infantry International" in 2023 to establish new standards in the training of light infantry forces. Night combat plays a central role in his training system. The former infantry officer was particularly influenced by his deployments with the Royal Marines (UK), the Telemark Bataljon (NOR), and in Kabul. The specialist author has been writing articles on infantry topics since 2013 and is the author of BLACK BOOK 2 "The Tactical Drone".

lightinfantry.de
patreon.com/lightinfantryinternational

APPENDIX

THE FIGHT FOR THE INIATIVE
BY VALERIJ ZALUSCHNYJ

The mass use of drones—for persistent reconnaissance or as FPV kamikaze bombers—is the most striking feature of the war in Ukraine so far.

THE FIGHT FOR THE INIATIVE

VALERII ZALUZHNYI

A few days before his dismissal in February 2024, Valerii Zaluzhnyi, then Commander-In-Chief of the Ukrainian armed forces, published an up-to-minute article. In it, he described the transformation of the war in Ukraine and analyzed the country's need to adapt in order to continue defending itself successfully.

ON THE MODERN DESIGN OF MILITARY OPERATIONS IN THE RUSSO–UKRAINIAN WAR: THE FIGHT FOR THE INITIATIVE

Almost eighty years separate us from the last battles of World War II, which became the basis of the strategic vision for war in the late twentieth and early twenty-first centuries.

Despite the rapid development of weapons and equipment, namely aviation, missiles and space assets, the development of communications and electronic warfare, the strategy for victory was to destroy the enemy and capture or liberate their territory. The achievement of this victory strategy directly relied on the level of development and the number of weapons used, determining the forms and methods employed. Of course, knowledge of the basics of strategy, operational art, and tactics should accompany the career growth of military specialists and solve two primary to respond effectively to a situation that requires rising to the occasion, countering the enemy, weakening their forces, and gaining time to take control. This entire process carries significant risks and uncertainties because there is only one opportunity to oppose enemy forces effectively with limited resources.

In my view, the primary task is to promptly identify the war-related requirements for advancing technological progress and consequently rapidly developing weapons, equipment, the global and domestic political situations, and the economic landscape. Therefore, it is crucial to identify a unique approach and reasoning for each conflict, enabling the exploration of novel techniques to adapt to new situations and attain victory.

When it comes to our own strategy, we cannot completely disregard existing doctrines that explain how to plan and execute operations. We just need to understand that we will continuously change and update them with new content.

The principles of operational art will remain unchanged. Therefore, considering the requirements of today, our most important task will be to **adopt a new approach to the forms and methods of using the Defense Forces** to achieve victory.

The **main reason for the change** in the strategy, forms and methods of employment of forces, of course, is the development of new weapons and equipment–especially unmanned systems, the use of which has become widespread and enables the performance of a wide, and ever growing, range of tasks. Hence, unmanned systems, along with other cutting-edge weapons, serve as the primary means to disengage from prolonged positional military operations, which are not advantageous for Ukraine for multiple reasons.

In the current situation, there are still several factors that undoubtedly influence the decision to search for new forms of employment of the defence forces. Here are some of them:

▶ unstable political situation around Ukraine, which leads to a reduction in military support.
▶ high probability of Russia provoking several conflicts following the example of Israel and Yemen that distract key partners from supporting Ukraine.
▶ exhaustion of our partners' stocks of missiles and ammunition for artillery and air defence because of the high intensity of hostilities in Ukraine and the impossibility of their rapid production against the background of the global shortage of propellant charges.
▶ insufficient effectiveness of the sanctions policy, resulting in the full deployment of the capacity of the military-industrial complex in Russia and its partner states, which allows them to successfully wage a positional war of attrition.
▶ a significant advantage in the mobilization of human resources of the enemy and the inability of state institutions in Ukraine to improve the state of manning

of the Defence Forces without the use of unpopular measures.

▶ imperfection of the regulatory framework governing the military-industrial complex in our country, and partial monopolization of this industry leading to difficulties in the production of domestic ammunition– resulting in the deepening of Ukraine's dependence on allies.

▶ The complexity involved in determining the priorities of support from our allies creates uncertainty about how the armed struggle will unfold on such a large scale.

The combat operations conducted by the Ukrainian Armed Forces, particularly in the years 2022-2023, are unparalleled and continue to be our exclusive legacy. Therefore, in our constant pursuit of victory, it is necessary to continuously assess our existing capabilities, as the outcome of combat operations relies on them. Additionally, we must constantly seek ways to gain an advantage over the enemy. By understanding the outcome of battles, we can identify the circumstances in which the enemy will cease further aggression. Creating these circumstances is seen as an effective utilization of the resources in the Ukrainian Armed Forces' arsenal. Considering the factors mentioned above and the current conditions of warfare, the best approach to gain an advantage may be to fully master a range of affordable, modern, and highly efficient assets that are rapidly advancing. The utilization of advancements in technology is crucial for achieving victory in scientific, technical, technological, and tactical battles. Furthermore, it will result in resource preservation and savings for both Ukraine and our partners.

There is a strong need to enhance the capabilities of unmanned systems and other advanced technologies in order to have a positive impact on the progress of conflicts. As a result, there is a growing interest in exploring new forms and methods of utilization, which will inevitably lead to changes in the structure of the Ukrainian Armed Forces and other defense components.

It is possible to **increase the impact of UAS and other new systems** on the effectiveness of combat operations due to:

▶ Enhancing commanders' situational awareness by enabling real-time monitoring and maintaining it 24/7 in all weather conditions.
▶ Real-time maintenance and monitoring of fires and strikes 24/7.
▶ Conducting accurate and precise strikes on enemy forces and their facilities, whether they are on the front lines or deeper in enemy territory.

Therefore, it is crucial to develop a new operational design using current technology. This design should focus not only on the spatial and temporal aspects of military operations but also on creating favorable conditions and achieving specific effects that will help accomplish the operation's objective.

Considering **combat experience** and the projected evolu-
tion of armed conflict, the following conditions are crucial:

▶ Attaining complete air supremacy, particularly at al-
   titudes that allow for effective combat, intelligence,
   surveillance, and logistics.
▶ Preventing the enemy from engaging in offensive or
   defensive actions.
▶ Improving the maneuverability of our own troops
   while effectively immobilizing the enemy forces.
▶ Establishing a safe pathway to specific lines and gaining authority over critical terrain.

At first sight, these conditions are clearly conservative
and traditional, emphasizing the use of established forms
and methods. However, this perception is only superfi-
cial, as the means of attaining these goals have already
undergone transformations. Sadly, the previous assets
are gradually turning into an unattainable aspiration for
the Ukrainian Armed Forces. The primary priority is now
to adapt the strategies to achieve these objectives.

By adhering to the proposed notion of establishing
definitive conditions, the process of accomplishing them
will inherently involve addressing multiple operational
tasks, wherein the necessary outcomes will be produced
through the effective utilization of allocated resources. It
is important for them to diverge from the usual template
and align with the current doctrine, even if it means
compromising on technological superiority.

Undoubtedly, the creation of essential effects is already causing significant changes in the way forces are employed. Consequently, in order to effectively achieve the desired effects, it is essential to treat the following factors as separate entities today:

▶ **Managing the digital battlefield.**
▶ **Managing radio-electronic situational awareness.**
▶ **Combined operations employing unmanned aerial vehicles and cyber assets for attack purposes.**
▶ **Handling logistical operations.**

All the operations mentioned are already being mastered and enhanced. All these tasks follow a common concept and plan, ensuring coordination and interconnection, while having distinct variations in their content.

When it comes to executing operations to achieve desired outcomes, we can assume that they will primarily have a defensive or offensive nature. However, when considering the actual methods employed, we can categorize them as follows:

▶ **Operations to diminish the economic strength of the adversary.**
▶ **Autonomous seek and strike operations.**
▶ **Implementing autonomous operations to manage crisis areas.**
▶ **Attack assets conducting psychological operations.**
▶ **Utilizing technology for contactless defensive operations.**

As the assets continue to develop, the list of operations will gradually expand, leading to revisions in doctrinal documents and the emergence of a completely new philosophy for preparing and conducting hostilities. Combining or introducing new independent operations will require the creation of a new organizational structure. The key to achieving all of this is the ability of state institutions to respond flexibly and rapidly to changes.

Consequently, the conventional defensive, offensive, and stabilization operations have undergone a transformation that departs from the traditional linear and template-oriented methods of planning and conducting these operations, changing their fundamental characteristics and substance. Simultaneously, these operations were essentially combined, taking into account the perspectives of partners. Additionally, in modern circumstances, we reinterpret the well-established concept of **network-centric warfare** as achieving desired outcomes and critical conditions through the utilization of appropriate capabilities, rather than relying solely on troop operations.

Additionally, it is worth mentioning that unmanned and other advanced technological systems have the capability to improve combat operations and effectively address various organizational challenges faced by the Defence Forces of Ukraine:

- ▶ Optimize the use of remote-controlled assets to decrease losses and promote non-contact operations.
- ▶ Decrease the reliance on traditional weaponry in military missions.
- ▶ Ensure that the hostilities are conducted with minimal reliance on heavy military machinery.
- ▶ Even without a strong Navy, we aim to achieve efficient and low-risk victories against enemy surface and submarine forces, as well as their coastal infrastructure, across the entire theater of operations at sea.
- ▶ Achieve significant and swift damage to critical infrastructure and communication networks through alternative, cost-efficient means, bypassing the use of expensive missiles and manned aircraft.

The list of advantages provided is not comprehensive and is likely to evolve, thus broadening the scope of employment possibilities. Naturally, during a military conflict, the opposing forces will seek strategies to defend themselves and gain the upper hand. Hence, in light of the advancements in attack systems, including unmanned ones, it becomes crucial to enhance protection and counteraction systems.

Therefore, in order to become proficient in new forms and techniques, the Defence Forces must establish an entirely new state system for technological modernization, comprising the following subsystems:

- ▶ Advancement and assistance in scientific research.
- ▶ Manufacturing and maintenance.
- ▶ Incorporating and utilizing combat experience in all training.
- ▶ Mobilization of troops.
- ▶ Financing solutions that are adaptable.
- ▶ Strategic planning and implementing efficient logistics.

In all likelihood, future research and development efforts will need to be dedicated to each subsystem individually. Nevertheless, it is evident that the system should be holistic and flexible, allowing for the inclusion of different entities, financial factors, and production adjustments. There is no doubt that this will require some time, but it is the time factor that is crucial.

Taking into account the existing framework for deploying forces, technological advancements, command and control systems, past experiences, and input from our partners, it could potentially require a time span of around five months to develop a new system that meets the required operational capability. The reason for this term is the requirement to establish suitable organizational structures, allocate personnel and equipment, provide training for personnel, ensure resource support, develop necessary infrastructure, manage logistics, and establish a doctrinal framework.

Taking this into account, our **main priorities for 2024** should be:

- ▶ Establishing a sophisticated infrastructure to ensure the Defense Forces receive high-tech resources.
- ▶ Introducing a novel approach to preparing and conducting hostilities that takes probable limitations into consideration.
- ▶ The objective is to rapidly gain proficiency in new capabilities for conducting military operations.

We are discussing the fact that, in today's world, the Armed Forces of Ukraine, along with other components of the State Security Forces, have the ability not only to defeat the enemy but also to ensure the preservation of the nation. Hence, it is of utmost importance to capitalize on the opportunities presented by the changing war conditions. This will help us maximize the accumulation of advanced combat capabilities, allowing us to use fewer resources to deal significant blows to the enemy, halt their aggression, and protect Ukraine from future threats.

Valerii Zaluzhnyi,
Commander-in-Chief

VALERII ZALUZHNYI

was Commander-in-Chief of the Ukrainian Army from July 2021 to February 2024. He earned the reputation as the man behind his country's military success, which Russia attacked in February 2022. The article "The Fight for the Initiative" appeared a few days before his dismissal. Zaluzhnyi pursued a decentralized and flexible way of waging war. He developed the vision of a Ukrainian Army that could think and make decentralized decisions and maneuver independently to win against Russia.

SPARTANAT

www.spartanat.com

SPARTANAT

**MILITARY NEWS
TACTICAL LIFE
GEAR & REVIEWS**

OUR WORLD
LINKTR.EE/SPARTANAT